CONTENTS

NORMAN POOLE

Miles of split rail fences can be seen along the Parkway.

Every fact has been checked in order to ensure that this book is as up to date as possible at press time. Details such as phone numbers, hours and prices are subject to change, so please check ahead. The publisher accepts no responsibility for any consequences arising from the use of this book. We welcome suggestions from readers. Please write to: Editor, Leisure Publishing Company, 3424 Brambleton Ave., P.O. Box 21535, Roanoke, VA 24018

Cover photos courtesy Pat & Chuck Blackley, Ronnie Luttrell, Bill Carter, Nye Simmons. Facing page: The Blue Ridge Parkway around MP 450 in North Carolina. Photo by Ronnie Luttrell.

Virginia's Shenandoah Valley — Winchester, Front Royal
Harrisonburg
Staunton
Virginia's Blue Ridge Highlands — Lexington, Charlottesville
Roanoke
Bedford
Virginia's Jefferson Country
Northeast Tennessee
Wytheville
Kingsport
Johnson City
North Carolina's High Country
Knoxville
Asheville
Tennessee Smokies — Cherokee
North Carolina's Blue Ridge/Asheville
North Carolina Smokies

How to Use This Guide

This guidebook's focus is the Blue Ridge Parkway, the Smokies, and nearby areas. Opening pages offer an overview, map, wildlife and events. Following are eight regional sections. Last are guides to lodging, trails, shopping, additional attractions, visitor centers, weather and blooms.

All pages relating to each region have color-coded thumb tabs.

1 Introduction
Presents landscape, history and character of each region as well as what it has to offer the visitor.

A **locator map** shows where you are in relation to the entire region.

2 Pictorial Map
Shows the Parkway network and gives an illustrated overview of the whole region. Places to visit are numbered. There is also information on noteworthy aspects of the region.

3 Detailed Information
Important towns and other places to visit are described individually. They are listed in general order of Parkway milepost, running from north to south following the numbering on the *Pictorial Map*. Within each town or city there is information on sites and sights.

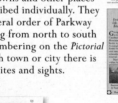

Screened **story boxes** give sponsored information on the region.

4 Detailed Traveler-Needs Information
Lodging and dining information is provided in sponsored capsule format.

Abbreviations Key
MP – Blue Ridge
    Parkway Milepost
& – Handicapped
    accessible
FAX – Fax services
    available
Credit cards –
    MC-MasterCard,
    V-Visa, DC-Diners
    Club, AE-
    American Express

Historic sites.

Mabry Grist Mill

Spend the night. Grab a bite.

While you're visiting the Blue Ridge Parkway's famous historic sites, stop along the way and enjoy comfortable lodging, rustic cabins, unique gift shops and Parkway-favorite restaurants.

Bluffs Lodge

Bluffs Lodge Restaurant & Gift Shop

Crabtree Meadows Snack Bar & Gift Shop

Mabry Mill Restaurant & Gift Shop
276.952.2947 **MP 176**
　Rustic cabin rentals: 540.593.3503

Bluffs Lodge, Restaurant & Gift Shop
336.372.4499 **MP 241**

Crabtree Meadows Snack Bar & Gift Shop
828.675.4236 **MP 339**

BlueRidgeResort.com

All properties open seasonally, May through October only.
Please call ahead for hours of operation.

FOREVER ✦ RESORTS

Forever Resorts is an Authorized Concessioner of the National Park Service.

 p. 51   p. 65   Please refer to map p. 51

Putting the Parkway/ Smokies Region on the Map

The Blue Ridge Parkway begins at MP 0 between Waynesboro and Afton in Virginia, at the southern end of the 105 miles of Skyline Drive and Shenandoah National Park. The Parkway's terminus is at MP 469 in western North Carolina in the Great Smoky Mountains National Park.

The Parkway is 469 miles of easy driving through beautiful, ever-changing vistas known far and wide for careful preservation and the great variety of its natural forms.

◇ **Parkway Visitation:**

The Blue Ridge Parkway avages 20 million visitors per year.

Visitation builds during tspring and into summer, an peaks in October, when 2 3 million people visit.

Statistics have been kepvisitation since 1939, whejust over 100,000 people on the roadway. The all-timhigh was just over 25 millicin 1988, as the Parkway enjoyed a swell perhaps

KEY

▬ Blue Ridge Parkway

▬ Skyline Drive

⑧⑴ Interstates

㉒㉑ U.S. Highways

▭ Rivers

MP Parkway Milepost

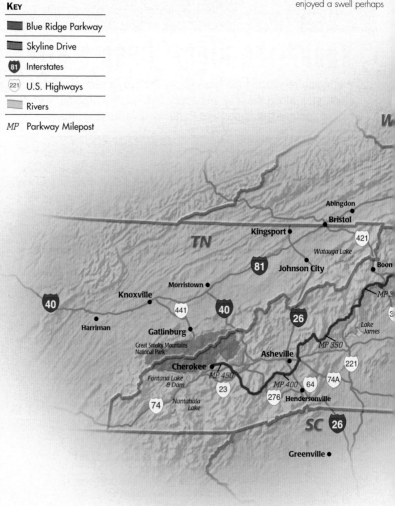

Scale is approximate only

1 inch = about 50 miles

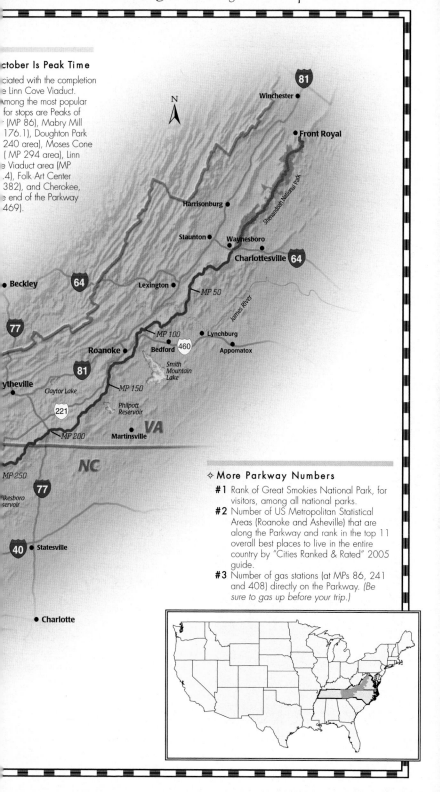

ctober Is Peak Time

ciated with the completion
e Linn Cove Viaduct.
mong the most popular
for stops are Peaks of
(MP 86), Mabry Mill
176.1), Doughton Park
240 area), Moses Cone
(MP 294 area), Linn
e Viaduct area (MP
.4), Folk Art Center
382), and Cherokee,
e end of the Parkway
469).

N

Winchester ●

● Front Royal

Shenandoah National Park

Harrisonburg ●

Staunton ●   Waynesboro ●

Charlottesville **64**

● Beckley   **64**   Lexington ●   — *MP 50*

James River

77

77   — *MP 100*   ● Lynchburg

Roanoke ●   Bedford ● **460**

Appomatox ●

Smith Mountain Lake

ytheville   Claytor Lake   — *MP 150*

81

221

Philpott Reservoir

— *MP 200*   Martinsville ●   *VA*

NC

MP 250

77

lkesboro servoir

40 ● Statesville

● Charlotte

✧ More Parkway Numbers

#1 Rank of Great Smokies National Park, for visitors, among all national parks.

#2 Number of US Metropolitan Statistical Areas (Roanoke and Asheville) that are along the Parkway and rank in the top 11 overall best places to live in the entire country by "Cities Ranked & Rated" 2005 guide.

#3 Number of gas stations (at MPs 86, 241 and 408) directly on the Parkway. *(Be sure to gas up before your trip.)*

The Parkway: A Look Back & Along The Road

The Blue Ridge Parkway today is in many ways what it has been for all its years – a ribbon of highway along the high Appalachian ridges of the Southeast, and a gateway to the discovery of ways of life that thrive along its pristine miles.

Big sky vistas overlooking gorgeous farmland are a large part of the parkway's attraction to visitors.

The Blue Ridge Parkway winds its way for 469 miles of beautiful ridgeline, from Waynesboro, Va. to Cherokee, N.C. The two-lane, 45-mph, limited access roadway generally rides over or ducks under the big state and national highways, with only occasional crossings of state or U.S. highways.

There's a simple, Spartan feel as you drive – so clean and green as to be a park. Which of course it is.

There are no commercial signs here – just the small, tidy, white-letters-on-brown-field necessaries pertaining to distances and crossing – and an occasional new curve-ahead sign.

The parkway wends its way through many historical areas, giving visitors the chance to learn about Appalachian life through the ages.

The miracle that is the Blue Ridge Parkway begins with its setting. Here in the Southeastern U.S. – that highly populated, technologically advanced and increasingly urbanized home to more than half the nation's people – there's a blue ribbon of magic, a linear park once referred to as having been "painted with a comet's tail."

It's a roadway – just hours from the big metropolises of Washington, D.C. and Atlanta and Charlotte – that's embraced by trees and other green, interrupted here and there with a pullover to look at more distant trees and other green.

The seed of this wonder goes back to the 1930s, when economic and social forces converged with natural ones to create a need in all those realms.

With the Great Depression, many people needed work, and part of the work created by President Franklin Roosevelt's New Deal was the making of parks.

Twin Tunnels, near MP 345, is emblematic of the grace of the parkway's 26 tunnels, most of which are in North Carolina.

those parks as well as other significant spots along the roadway, including restrooms, gasoline and highway crossings is found on the next page.

While You're on the Parkway...

- Speed limit is 45 mph.
- Pets must be leashed.
- Harming animals and harvesting plants are prohibited.
- Stay on trails; park only in designated areas.
- Weather can close parts of the Parkway at times; call (828) 298-0398 to check.
- For safety or traffic problems call (800) PARKWATCH.

Miles of unspoiled hardwood forest and fall foliage can be viewed at the many overlooks, such as this one at Chestoa (MP 320).

A young landscape architect named Stanley Abbott came south from building a linear park in New York state and went to work on a vision to create a series of recreational parks along the Parkway's complete length – what Abbott called "beads on a string – the rare gems in the necklace."

The legacy of that vision is the existence – at an average of 30-40 miles apart – of the parks and recreational sites that are one of the major draws of the Parkway.

A mile-by-mile overview of

Parkway Anchors: Visit Two Mountain Cities

The Parkway is anchored by the two largest cities along its miles – Roanoke, Va., near MP 120 and Asheville, N.C., near MP 382.

Roanoke, former home of Parkway headquarters, is known for its vibrant downtown, its century-old open-air farmers' market and its national-model cultural center. www.visitroanokeva.com.

Asheville, home of the Parkway's new headquarters building, is also the site of the majestic Biltmore Estate, the venerable Grove Park Inn and a thriving downtown. www.exploreasheville.com.

The mountains of the south are famed for their rhododendrons and azaleas. A schedule of blooms can be found on page 145.

Did You Know?

• The highest point on the Parkway is at Richland Balsam, N.C., at MP 417.1, where the elevation is 6,047 feet above sea level.

• The highest point on the Virginia miles is at MP 76.5, at 3,950 feet.

• The lowest point is at Otter Creek, Va. (MP 63.2), with an elevation of 649 feet.

• Most the Parkway's 469 miles ride atop 355 miles of the Blue Ridge mountains; the remaining miles move through the Blacks, the Great Craggies, Pisgah Ledge and the Great Balsams.

• Though the Parkway was largely complete by 1967, the very last section – the Linn Cove Viaduct (MP 304.4) beneath Grandfather Mountain – was not completed until 1987.

• Farms border the parkway for much of its length. Today some farmers lease Parkway land for pasture or crops, while others maintain a scenic easement,

keeping the land uncultivated.

• Most of the split-rail fences you see along the parkway are made of chestnut. Examples of snake, post and rail, buck, and picket fences can be found at Groundhog Mountain (MP 189).

• The 26 tunnels on the Parkway were cut through a total of 2.25 miles of solid rock, and they range in length from the 150-foot Rough Ridge Tunnel (MP 349) to the 1,434-foot Pine Mountain Tunnel (MP 399.1).

Small roadside farmers' stands are an excellent way to sample some of the fine local produce, especially apples during the fall season.

Road Conditions...

Call the park information line, (828) 298-0398 for road closures by section and access to parkway weather reports.

Two sections of the parkway between Linville Falls and Mount Mitchell are closed as of press time after almost 50 inches of rain fell in western North Carolina in September 2004. By summer 2005 these sections are expected to be open.

The Appalachians have a rich history of music with a wide variety of folk influences.

Milepost	food	visitor center	comfort station	gas	picnic area	campground	trails
MP 0 – U.S. 250. *Rockfish Gap.*		✓					
MP 5.8 – *Humpback Rocks.* An outdoor museum containing log buildings from a century ago.		✓	✓		✓		✓
MP 29 – *Whetstone Ridge*							
MP 45.6 – U.S. 60.							
MP 60.9 – *Otter Creek.* Along Otter Creek.	✓		✓			✓	✓
MP 63.8 – *James River.* Restored canal lock and exhibits.		✓	✓		✓		✓
MP 63.9 – U.S. 501.							
MP 86 – *Peaks of Otter.* Lake, gift shop.	✓	✓	✓	✓	✓	✓	✓
MP 95.9 – U.S. 460.							
MP 115 – *Virginia's Explore Park.* Frontier life exhibits, interpretive center, biking trails (1.5-mile spur)	✓	✓	✓				
MP 120.4 – *Roanoke Mountain.* Link to campground and Roanoke.			✓			✓	✓
MP 121.4 – U.S. 220.							
MP 154.5 – *Smart View.* A 500-acre recreation area.			✓		✓		✓
MP 169 – *Rocky Knob Recreation Area.* Cabins.		✓	✓		✓	✓	✓
MP 176.1 – *Mabry Mill.* Gristmill, exhibits, souvenirs.	✓		✓				✓
MP 177.7 – U.S. 58.							
MP 188.8 – *Groundhog Mountain.* Fences, observation tower.			✓				
MP 199.4 – U.S. 52.							
MP 217.5 – *Cumberland Knob Recreation Area.*		✓	✓		✓		✓
MP 229.7 – U.S. 21.							
MP 238.5 – *Brinegar Cabin.* An 1880s log cabin.							✓
MP 241.1 – *Doughton Park.* Lodging, gift shop.	✓		✓	✓	✓	✓	✓
MP 258.6 – *Northwest Trading Post.*		✓	✓				
MP 272 – *E.B. Jeffress Park.*			✓		✓		✓
MP 276.6 – U.S. 421.							
MP 291.9 – U.S. 321.							
MP 294.1 – *Moses Cone Memorial Park.* Magnificent home, fishing, horseback riding, craft center.		✓	✓				✓
MP 297.1 – *Julian Price Memorial Park*			✓		✓	✓	✓
MP 304.4 – *Linn Cove Viaduct*		✓	✓				✓
MP 316.4 – *Linville Falls*		✓	✓		✓	✓	✓
MP 317.5 – U.S. 221.							
MP 331 – *Museum of North Carolina Minerals.* Exhibits.		✓	✓				
MP 339.5 – *Crabtree Meadows.* Gift shop, Crabtree Falls.	✓		✓		✓		✓
MP 364.6 – *Craggy Gardens Visitor Center.* Exhibits.		✓	✓		✓	✓	✓
MP 382 – *Folk Art Center.* Crafts, gallery, demonstrations.		✓	✓				
MP 382.4 – U.S. 70.							
MP 384.7 – U.S. 74A.							
MP 388.1 – U.S. 25.							
MP 407.6/408.8 – *Mount Pisgah.*	✓	✓	✓	✓	✓	✓	✓
MP 411.9 – U.S. 276.							
MP 443.1 – U.S. 19A.							
MP 451.2 – *Waterrock Knob.* Exhibits.		✓	✓				✓
MP 455.7 – U.S. 19.							

The trails in blue are wheelchair-accessible.

Parkway History: A '30s Serendipity

The combined forces of the Great Depression and a great vision for public spaces came together in the 1930s to allow the building of a unique American treasure.

"The Parkway... has but one real reason for existence, which is to please by revealing the charm and interest of the native American countryside..." That's how original Blue Ridge Parkway landscape architect Stanley Abbott articulated his vision.

Stanley Abbott was the Parkway's first landscape architect.

Setting the Stage

Several events conspired to set the stage for the building of the Blue Ridge Parkway. Two new national parks – Shenandoah National Park in Virginia and Great Smoky Mountains National Park in North Carolina and Tennessee – needed a road to link them. The Great Depression provided large numbers of unemployed workers as well as a pool of highly trained but temporarily idled engineers and landscape architects.

After much debate among the politicians of Virginia, North Carolina and Tennessee, the location was decided, and construction of the Blue Ridge Parkway began on September 11, 1935.

The Design

When young Stanley Abbott was appointed resident landscape architect for the new park-to-park road, he applied his diverse skills and experience to convert 469 miles of hodge-podge mountain land into the nation's most famous rural national parkway, conforming to "a proper road's" guidelines: (1) Lie easily on the ground; (2) Blend harmoniously with the topography; (3) Appear as if it had grown out of the soil.

He designed not only a parkway but a total recreation program, incorporating visitor centers, hiking trails, lodges, campgrounds, milepost markers, interpretive programs, visitor services and lodges. He viewed these entities as a series of "parks" scattered throughout the length of the route.

Blue Ridge Parkway tunnels were built with stone gathered close to the roadway.

The Construction

The Parkway was built in sections that were then connected, with construction commencing in areas where the right-of-way had been acquired and where people desperately needed to work.

Like most of the country in the wake of the Depression, the Blue Ridge region was economically depressed, and the idea of a paved road passing through this relatively undeveloped region appealed to many mountain residents. Yet some resentment began to grow, with many who sold land for the Parkway objecting to the road's bisecting their farmlands. In most cases, ill will gradually changed to approval as Parkway neighbors grew to appreciate the road as an economic, recreational and cultural resource.

The Missing Link

One by one the road sections and parks were completed until only one unit – the route around Grandfather Mountain in North

Haystacks were a commonly placed feature of the early years of the parkway.

Carolina – remained unfinished.

After years of stalemate, the park service masterminded a compromised middle route between the park service's "high route" and the landowner's "low route." The route utilized state-of-the-art engineering to build an ingenious bridge aesthetically blended into the mountain. The Linn Cove Viaduct was built literally from the top down minimizing disturbance to the natural environment.

In 1987, when the famed Linn Cove Viaduct was dedicated, the 469 miles were at last rendered one long, beautiful park through the Appalachians.

Civilian Conservation Corps crews contributed significantly to the building of the Parkway.

Nature's "Edge" Along The Parkway

The Blue Ridge Parkway is a perfect example and provider of "edge habitat" – the transition area between deep forest and open field. It's in these areas where you're most likely to see the parkway's most abundant animals.

The white-tailed deer along the parkway grow from this shy and retiring youth to become outgoing and curious about Parkway travelers.

Travelers find the Blue Ridge Parkway a perpetual zoo, because with 469 miles of "edge," even nearing age 70, it's still full of life.

Born in 1935 in the Depression, the 80,000 acres of parkway property host more than 20 million visitors a year, providing not only multi-hued wildflowers and panoramic vistas, but bounding deer, barreling groundhog, scooting ruffed grouse, soaring hawk, flitting song birds (nearly 100 species during spring migrations), with dashes of gobbler, skunk and cottontail thrown in.

King of this road is the white-tailed deer. See enough of him and you conclude deer are gregarious and curious, especially about vehicles. They hang around, or double back, to check out a car they've noticed, or escaped, seconds before.

The wily groundhog, can pop up anywhere. Elusive, comical and fearful, this rotund blob of reddish-brown fur is tall on instinct, short on smarts.

If you get between 'hogs and their escape routes, they'll improvise: crawl into a retaining wall drainage pipe at Craven's Gap (Mile 377) or snuggle into an embankment depression near Grassy Knob tunnel (MP 397).

Bonas Umbellus, the ruffed grouse, shows up along the road during the March-April breeding season, its feathers fluffing, its body expanding from crown to toe like some pompous orator-to-be.

On May 16, 1995, just south of Linville Falls (MP 319, 321), two grouse accosted me with an even greater reluctance to escape than usual; in fact they walked the pavement oblivious to the dangers of moving vehicles. Determined to stand pat, they paced across the road eerily in slow motion, at times glancing skyward, but always seeming mindful to some hidden duty – perhaps in the brush, or to a dozen little balls of bird, a set of fluffy chicks. Sometimes these chicks scoot into the road, where mama seems to say to you, "Slow down for my babies; they're precious."

The groundhog is an edge habitat classic: often visible, always quick to beat a hasty retreat from view.

Ruffed grouse may be trailed along the roadside for some distance without flushing.

One of the most prepossessing critters of the edge is the wild turkey. Turkey hotspots emerge just south of Cumberland Knob. In mid-June gobblers peck the roadside (MP 218), a hen guiding her chicks (MP 224) off the edge into woods.

Another critter flees when smelling danger, but not because it has a stripe up its back. On my Night of the Five Skunks, these little headlight-shy animals skitter mincingly across the road, fall into a escape route – a narrow, shallow ditch toward the safety of a concrete drain. One swirls briefly in the glow of a pressing car, revealing its white stripe, as if to say: "Don't mess with me, or I'll let you have it."

A perfect "edge effect" practitioner is the eastern cottontail. Although speedy afoot, it may freeze to avoid notice. This makes them perfect models

for a photograph. You'd think they'd consider humans more threatening than the snakes that await them under cover in this habitat.

The "edge," where different food and cover types meet, like grassy glades running through deciduous woodlands or high-altitude evergreen forests – a paved road bisecting it all is perfect habitat for a variety of birds. The Parkway offers a never-ending supply, from the American bittern to the whip-poor-will. The annual autumn hawk migration down the Blue Ridge can be spectacular. Some good hawk-watching spots are at MP 0, 45.7, 95.3, 168, 235, 364.1, 404.5 and 422.4. Birds seen in all seasons include cardinal, Carolina chickadee, red-tailed hawk, tufted titmouse, pileated and red-bellied woodpecker, and the Carolina wren.   —*Bill Weekes*

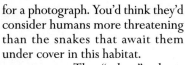

June (early June through the third week) brings spectacular shows of Catawba rhododendron. Two of the best places to view their beauty are the Craggy Gardens and Linville Falls areas.
Other rhododendron and azalea varieties: Rosebay rhododendron is the larger, white variety (mid to late June into July) around Rocky Knob, Va. Flame azalea and pink azalea (early to late May) is in many areas. Mountain laurel (mid to late June and into July) blooms in higher elevations.

The red-bellied woodpecker can often be heard tapping away at trees.

Fairs and Festivals: The Year's Best

All year long, cities and towns along the Blue Ridge Parkway host wonderful events – from quilt shows to battle re-enactments. Here's a small sampling. For a complete list of Parkway/Smokies events, visit www.blueridgecountry.com.

SPRING

Virginia's Shenandoah Valley
Skyline Drive MP 0-Parkway MP 135

Highland Maple Festival
March 12-13, 19-20.
Monterey. Crafts, clogging, music. (540) 468-2550.

Strawberry Festival
May 6-May 7. Roanoke.
Crafts, desserts and strawberries. (540) 563-5036.

Virginia's Jefferson Country
Skyline Drive MP 80-Parkway MP 116

Celtic Festival/Irish Music Concert
April 23. Sedalia Center, Big Island. Irish food and drink. (434) 299-5080.

Virginia Wine Festival
May 21-22. Ash Lawn-Highland, Charlottesville.
Crafts, music, children's activities. (434) 293-9539.

Virginia's Blue Ridge Highlands
Parkway MP 116-216.9

16 Hands Studio Tour
May 7-8, Nov. 25-27. Floyd and Montgomery counties.
Artists in pottery and wood. (540) 745-3595.

Devotees gather at Civil War re-enactments all over the mountains to re-create battles.

Ralph Stanley Memorial Bluegrass Festival
May 26-28. Hills of Home Park, Coeburn. Bluegrass, camping. (276) 395-6318.

North Carolina's High Country
MP 216.9-337

MerleFest
April 28-May 1. Wilkesboro.
Music festival in memory of legend Doc Watson's son. (336) 838-6267.

Art in the Park
May 14, June 11, July 16, August 13, September 10, October 1. Blowing Rock.
Juried arts and crafts. (828) 295-7851.

North Carolina's Blue Ridge/Asheville
MP 312-423

Festival of Flowers at the Biltmore Estate
April 2-May 1. Asheville.
Live entertainment. (800) 543-2961.

Sandburg Folk Music Festival
May 30. Flat Rock. At the home of poet Carl Sandburg. (828) 693-4178.

North Carolina Smokies
MP 423-469

Great Smoky Mountain Trout Festival
May 21-22. Maggie Valley.
Carnival, entertainment, crafts. (828) 926-1686, (800) 624-4431.

Downtown Studio and Gallery Tour
June 18. Waynesville.
Walking tours, meet working artists. (828) 456-3517.

All ages enjoy dancing from square to circle to flat foot at regional festivals.

Tennessee Smokies
MP 469 and points west

A Mountain Quilt Festival
March 9-13. Pigeon Forge.
Lectures and seminars by national experts. (800) 251-9100.

Dogwood Arts Festival
April 8-24. Knoxville.
Tours, quilts, live entertainment. (865) 637-4561, (800) DOGWOOD.

Townsend in the Smokies Spring Festival and Old Timers Day
April 29-30, May 6-7.
Townsend. Bluegrass, storytelling, crafts. (800) 525-6834.

Northeast Tennessee
MP 469 and points north and west

Mac Tools Thunder Valley Nationals
April 29-May 1. Bristol.
NHRA championship drag race. (423) 764-1161.

Iris Festival
May 21-22. Greeneville.
Juried arts/crafts, entertainment. (423) 638-4111.

GO ON AND PAINT THE TOWN RED.

There's never been a better time to visit the Smokey Mountains and stay at Ramada, where you are guaranteed to get our best available rate, no questions asked.* However, if for some reason you manage to find a lower public rate 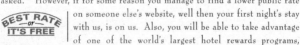 on someone else's website, well then your first night's stay with us, is on us. Also, you will be able to take advantage of one of the world's largest hotel rewards programs, TripRewards®**. Visit ramada.com for hotel details. For reservations or more information, visit us online or call today.

RAMADA.COM or 1.800.2 RAMADA

en español 1.888.709.4021

WIN
a Blue Ridge Mountain Getaway
to Virginia's Roanoke Valley.

*You can **WIN** this great prize by sending in the <u>FREE</u> Information Card at right.*

Enter today to win a Mountain Getaway! See prize details on page 19.

Experience the charm and beauty of Roanoke Valley! Located at the southern tip of the Shenandoah Valley, and conveniently situated off Interstate 81 at Exit 143 and the Blue Ridge Parkway at Milepost 120. Discover outdoor recreation, museums, attractions, farmers' markets, and unique shopping and restaurants.

Win three days and two nights at the historic Hotel Roanoke. This vintage 1882 hotel has been lovingly restored to its rich 19th century elegance and is listed in the National Register of Historic Places. Be our guest to 16 of the Valley's finest attractions including museums, living history, performing arts, natural wonders and a zoo. For the sports enthusiast, enjoy an Avalanche baseball game, ice skating and a round of golf for two at one of six mountainous golf courses. Come to the Roanoke Valley and experience Southern Hospitality Blue Ridge Mountain Style.

For more information about the area contact:
The Roanoke Valley Convention and Visitors Bureau
101 Shenandoah Avenue, NE Roanoke, Virginia 24016
For your FREE Guides call (800) 635-5535
or go to www.visitroanokeva.com

Fairs and Festivals: The Year's Best

SUMMER

Virginia's Shenandoah Valley
Skyline Drive MP 0-Parkway MP 135

Shenandoah Valley Music Festival
Various weekends July 22-30, Sept. 3-4. Orkney Springs. Big band, jazz, symphonic, folk. (800) 459-3396.

The Grandfather Mountain Highland Games are July 7-10.

VICKIE ROZEMA

Natural Chimney's Joust
Third Saturday in August. Mt. Solon. Jousting, bluegrass. (540) 350-2510.

Appalachian Folk Festival
September 24-25. Virginia's Explore Park, Roanoke. Storytellers, bluegrass, crafts. (800) 842-9163, (540) 427-1800.

Virginia's Jefferson Country
Skyline Drive MP 80-Parkway MP 116

Monticello Independence Day
July 4. Charlottesville. New U.S. residents take oath of citizenship. (434) 984-9822.

Virginia's Blue Ridge Highlands
MP 116-216.9

Virginia Highlands Festival
July 30-August 14. Abingdon. Music, theater, antiques, crafts. (276) 623-5266.

Old Fiddlers' Convention
August 8-13. Felt's Park, Galax. World's oldest and largest fiddlers' convention. (276) 236-8541.

North Carolina's High Country
MP 216.9-337

Rhododendron Festival
August 4-7. Bakersville. Street dancing, crafts, cars, fishing. (800) 227-3912.

WALTER KELLY PARRIS

North Carolina International Folk Festival (Folkmoot USA), celebrates world cultures.

Grandfather Mountain Highland Games
July 7-10. Linville. Scottish dance, music, athletics. (828) 733-1333.

North Carolina's Blue Ridge/Asheville
MP 312-423

Brevard Music Festival
June 22-August 7. Brevard Music Center. Jazz, Broadway, opera, symphony. (888) 384-8682.

Fairs and Festivals: The Year's Best

North Carolina Smokies
MP 423-469

Fourth of July Freedom Fest on the River
July 4. Riverfront Park, Bryson City. Crafts, food, fireworks. (828) 488-3681, (800) 867-9246.

North Carolina International Folk Festival
July 18-31. Waynesville. Dance, music and international cultures. (828) 452-2997.

Bluegrass music is featured at many festivals in the region.

Tennessee Smokies
MP 469 and points west

Celebrate Freedom Fest
August 13-20. Pigeon Forge. Music, dances, book talks. (865) 429-7350.

Gatlinburg Craftsmen's Fair
July 22-31, Oct. 6-23. Gatlinburg Convention Center. 180+ crafters. (865) 436-7479.

Northeast Tennessee
MP 469 and points north and west

Covered Bridge Celebration.
June 8-12. Elizabethon. Juried arts/crafts, bluegrass. (423) 547-3850.

Tennessee Quilts' Quiltfest 2004
July 21-23. Jonesborough and Johnson City. Workshops, classes. (423) 753-6644.

FALL

Virginia's Shenandoah Valley
Skyline Drive MP 0-Parkway MP 135

Shenandoah Valley Hot Air Balloon Festival
October 14-16. Historic Long Branch, Millwood. Crafts, wine tastings. (888) 558-5567.

Cedar Creek Living History and Re-enactment Weekend
October 15-16. Cedar Creek Battlefield, Middletown. Tours, drills, demonstrations. (540) 869-2064.

Virginia's Jefferson Country
Skyline Drive MP 80-Parkway MP 116

Virginia's Natural History Retreat Weekend
September 16-18. Wintergreen Nature Foundation, Nellysford. Guided hikes and workshops. (434) 325-7451.

Monticello Apple Tasting
October 22. Charlottesville. Tastings and discussions. (434) 984-9822.

Blue Ridge Folklife Festival is in Ferrum, Va. October 22.

Tennessee's Museum of Appalachia holds its annual Fall Homecoming October 6-9.

Virginia's Blue Ridge Highlands
MP 116-216.9

Grayson Highlands Fall Festival
September 24-25. Grayson Highlands State Park, Mouth of Wilson. Bluegrass, molasses, apple butter. (276) 773-3711.

Blue Ridge Folklife Festival
October 22. Blue Ridge Institute, Ferrum. Music, folklife demonstrations. (540) 365-4416.

North Carolina's High Country
MP 216.9-337

Valle Crucis Country Fair
October 15. Valle Crucis. Crafts, apple butter, entertainment. (828) 963-4609.

Oz Day and Harvest Fest
October 1-2. Beech Mountain. Meet the characters from Oz. (800) 468-5506, (828) 387-9283.

New River Festival
October 8. Todd. Music, crafts, family activities. (336) 877-1067.

Fairs and Festivals: The Year's Best

**Bascom Lamar
Lunsford Festival/
Madison County
Heritage Festival**
October 1. Mars Hill.
Music, dancing. (828)
689-5974.

**Craft Fair of the
Southern Highlands**
October 20-23. Folk Art
Center, Asheville.
Demonstrations, music.
(828) 298-7928.

Cherokee Indian Fair
October 4-8. Cherokee
Indian Fair Grounds,
Cherokee. A cultural cele-
bration. (828) 497-9195.

**John C. Campbell Folk
School Fall Festival**
October 1-2. Brasstown.
Regional artists.
(800) FOLK-SCH.

COURTESY PIGEON FORGE TOURISM

*Storytellers keep Applachian tales
alive in annual gatherings*

**18th-Century Trade
Faire**
September 10-11. Fort
Loudoun, Vonore. Colonial
history. (423) 884-6217.

**Tennessee Fall
Homecoming**
October 6-9. Museum
of Appalachia, Norris.
Music and crafts.
 (865) 494-7680.

**Unicoi County
Apple Festival**
October 7-8. Erwin.
Gospel, bluegrass,
crafts, food.
 (423) 743-3000.

**National
Storytelling Festival**
October 7-9.
Jonesborough.
The nation's oldest
storytelling event.
(423) 753-2171,
(800) 952-8392.

Jefferson County, West Virginia

Discover It All

Find out why Thomas
Jefferson said that the
view at Harpers Ferry was
worth crossing an ocean.

Less than an hour from
the Blue Ridge Parkway you
can experience ecotourism,
scenic beauty, and historical
heritage, ranging from the
Washington's of colonial
times, the Lewis & Clark
expedition to the Civil War.

Hike the Appalachian
Trail or bike the Antietam
Battlefield and C&O Canal.
Discover the best "birding"
spots or experience the

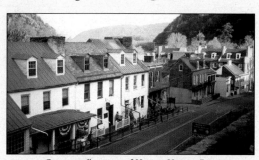

Go on a walking tour of Historic Harpers Ferry

thrill of Charles Town
Horse Racing and Slots.

Go on walking tours of
our historic towns. Take
time to shop our local
antiques and flea markets
or drive the 112 mile
Washington Heritage
Trail National Byway.

Traveler info:
Distance: 200 miles from
Parkway
For more info:
Jefferson County CVB
(866) Hello-WV
www.hello-WV.com

Enjoy rafting and tubing.

EASTERN GATEWAY
DISCOVER It-all!

West Virginia
Wild and Wonderful

1 *Please refer to map p.25*

Virginia's Shenandoah Valley

Skyline Drive MP 0 to MP 105; Parkway MP 0 to MP 135
Winchester • New Market • Harrisonburg • Staunton • Waynesboro • Lexington • Roanoke

The Shenandoah Valley's first natives had it right when they called this beautiful land "Daughter of the Stars." Sparkling rivers ramble through the land where small towns still host general stores, where centuries of history are still alive.

Virginia's long, gentle Shenandoah Valley is filled with the wonder of nature and the fun of outdoor recreation, with the creativity of art and the remembrance of history. Take a drive on Skyline Drive through Shenandoah National Park and see protected lands and wildlife. Or, drive to New Market Battlefield and revisit history. Tour Natural Bridge and see a wonder owned by Thomas Jefferson. Visit the thriving, historic small cities up and down the valley for urban fun. And between those cities are countless small towns equally full of history and heritage, and with placenames that resonate with the spirit of the region: Tom's Brook, Singers Glen, Shenandoah and Rockbridge Baths, to name but a few.

DOUGLAS MILLER

The downtown farmers' market in Roanoke (MP 105-125) sells produce, crafts and more year-round.

◁ *The hike to Little Stony Man near MP 39 on Skyline Drive is relatively easy with gorgeous views.*

The Monacan Indians considered Natural Bridge a sacred place. It's home to museums, a hotel and annual Easter sunrise services.

Getting Around

U.S. 11 and Interstate 81 run north-south in the valley, parallel to the Parkway and Skyline Drive, sometimes intersecting or merging, at times within sight of each other. U.S. 33 and 211 run east-west across the upper valley and both cross the Skyline Drive (as does the Appalachian Trail). U.S. 340 runs north-south between U.S. 11 and the Skyline Drive, on a rough parallel to those roadways. U.S. 250 slices across the valley in an east-west direction, cutting through Waynesboro and Staunton. U.S. 220, as it heads northwest out of Roanoke, makes a pretty drive toward West Virginia.

Key

▓	Blue Ridge Parkway
▓	Skyline Drive
▓	Highways
—	Secondary Roads
░	Rivers/Lakes
●	Overlooks
⁘	Tunnels
MP	Mileposts
🛢	Gasoline
♀♂	Restrooms
🍴	Food
⊼	Picnicking
▲	Visitor Center

•During the Civil War, the town of Winchester (birthplace of Willa Cather and Patsy Cline) switched hands between Confederate and Union control a total of 72 times.

•Grand Caverns, in Grottoes, has been open for tours the longest of any Virginia caves – since 1806.

•Architect Thomas U. Walter, who designed the U.S. Capitol dome, also designed the former Rockbridge County jail and Lexington Presbyterian Church.

The Appalachian Trail meanders its way through Shenandoah National Park.

TOM DIETRICH

PAT & CHUCK BLACKLEY

U.S. 11: The Old "Valley Pike"

Originally an animal path when humans began to settle in the valley, what is now U.S. 11 became a Native American trail, then a wagon road for European settlers. Today it is Main Street for many towns; in between it's scattered with echoes of yesteryear – antique shops, old roadside hotels, stone churches and family cemeteries.

N

Winchester

81

16   66

340   21   Front Royal

20

New Market   A

6   19   Luray   211

5

2

18   3

ynesboro

A

MP 5.8

10 miles

29

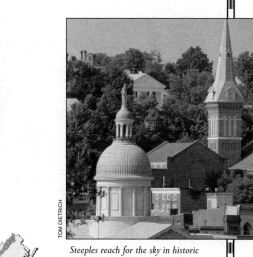

TOM DIETRICH

Steeples reach for the sky in historic Staunton, known for its beautiful architecture.

•George Washington first surveyed Natural Bridge in the 18th century; his initials are carved inside the great stone arch.

SIGHTS AND SITES AT A GLANCE

❶ Jefferson County, W.Va. (see p. 21)
❷ Shenandoah National Park
❸ Skyline Drive
❹ Glen Burnie House & Gardens
❺ Shenandoah River State Park
❻ New Market Battlefield State Historical Park
❼ George Washington and Jefferson National Forests
❽ Rockingham County
  ❽ ᴀ Courtyard by Marriott
  ❽ ʙ Harrisonburg

❾ Natural Chimneys
❿ Waynesboro
  ❿ ᴀ P. Buckley Moss Museum
⓫ Staunton
  ⓫ ᴀ Frontier Culture Museum
⓬ Lexington
⓭ Natural Bridge
⓮ Roanoke Valley
  ⓮ ᴀ Roanoke Valley Visitors Center
  ⓮ ʙ Hotel Roanoke & Conference Center
  ⓮ ᴄ Salem
⓯ Virginia's Explore Park

Caverns
  ⓰ Crystal Caverns at Hupp's Hill
  ⓱ Dixie Caverns
  ❻ ᴀ Endless Caverns
  ⓲ Grand Caverns
  ⓳ Luray Caverns
  ⓴ Shenandoah Caverns
  ㉑ Skyline Caverns

See also: Traveler Services p. 33 and Trip Planner Listings p. 130

White Oak Canyon falls, at milepost 42.6 of the Skyline Drive is one of the many waterfalls in Shenandoah National Park.

take Va. 340/522 north
•14 formal gardens surround the museum

Tour the circa 1794 home of Winchester's founder, Col. James Wood, including 25 acres of gardens. Since the mid-18th century, six generations of the same family have lived here. Today, the home is furnished with art and antiques collected by the last family member to live here, Julian Wood Glass, Jr. Also on the grounds is the new **Museum of the Shenandoah Valley**, which interprets the art, history and culture of the valley (www.shenandoahmuseum.org).

Shenandoah River State Park   ❺

Raymond R. "Andy" Guest Jr.
Shenandoah River State Park
350 Daughter of Stars Dr.
Bentonville, VA 22610
(540) 622-6840
shenandoahriver@dcr.state.va.us
www.dcr.state.va.us/parks/andygues.htm
•Leave the Skyline Drive at MP 0, Take Va. 340 south
•223 miles of water are designated for trout fishing

Shenandoah River State Park is more than 1,600 acres with 5.6 miles of river frontage along the south fork of the Shenandoah River. Most of the mountainous land is wooded. The park offers scenic vistas overlooking Massanutten Mountain to the west and Shenandoah National Park to the east. The river's south fork produces Class I and II rapids; the north fork is more sedate.

Shenandoah National Park   ❷

3655 U.S. Highway 211 East
Luray, VA 22835-9036
(540) 999-3500
www.nps.gov/shen
•MP 0 (to the north, the Parkway connects directly to Skyline Drive)
•Park includes more than 70 scenic overlooks – almost one per mile

Explore **Shenandoah National Park** by driving Skyline Drive or hiking, horseback riding or biking on more than 500 miles of trails, including 101 miles of the Appalachian Trail. There are peaks; Hawksbill and Stony Man are the park's highest. Waterfalls are abundant; Overall Run at 93 feet is the highest. Find traces of the mountain folk who lived here before it was a park. Spend the night at one of four campgrounds and enjoy watching the raccoon, deer and black bear that live here.

Skyline Drive   ❸

(540) 999-3500
www.nps.gov/shen
•MP 0 (to the north, the Parkway connects directly to Skyline Drive)

All 105 miles of Skyline Drive is contained within Shenandoah National Park which joins the Blue Ridge Parkway at Waynesboro, Va. Running from Front Royal to Waynesboro, Skyline Drive has accommodations and dining at Skyland and Big Meadows lodges. Most of the picnic areas, overlooks and landscaping were built by the Civilian Conservation Corps.

Glen Burnie House & Gardens   ❹

801 Amherst St., Rt. 50W
Winchester, VA 22601
(540) 662-1473
www.glenburniemuseum.org
•Leave Skyline Drive at MP 0,

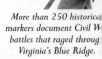

More than 250 historica[l] markers document Civil W[ar] battles that raged throug[h] Virginia's Blue Ridge.

New Market Battlefield State Historical Park ❻

8895 Collins Dr.
New Market, VA 22844
(540) 740-3101
nmbjw@shentel.net
www.vmi.edu/museum/nm
•Leave the Skyline Drive at MP 31.5, Take Va. 211 west
•The annual New Market Battle re-enactment attracts more than 2,000 Civil War re-enactors

257 Virginia Military Institute cadets fought in one of the last Confederate victories in the Shenandoah Valley at the 300-acre New Market Battlefield, which can be toured today, either staff-led or self-guided. The battle raged around the 19th-century **Bushong Farm**, which has been preserved. The **Hall of Valor Museum** is a memorial to the VMI cadets who fought.

The Shenandoah Valley is rich in Mennonite tradition.

George Washington and Jefferson National Forests ❼

5162 Valleypointe Pkwy.
Roanoke, VA 24019
(888) 265-0019
(540) 265-5100
www.southernregion.fs.fed.us/gwj

George Washington and Jefferson National Forests include more than a million acres of land with hiking, biking, water recreation and camping. The **Massanutten Visitors Center** at New Market has interpretive trails for blind and wheelchair-bound visitors. The **Sherman Gap Loop** follows some of the escape path George Washington planned to take during the Revolutionary War if he needed to retreat to Yorktown.

Rockingham County ❽

Harrisonburg-Rockingham Convention & Visitors Bureau
10 East Gay St.
Harrisonburg, VA 22802
(540) 434-2319
hrcvb@planetcomm.net
www.hrcvb.org/index.html
•U.S. 33 west intersects Skyline Drive at MP 65.5, Swift Run Gap
•Hiking, biking and camping abound in the county's 139,000 acres of national forest

Rockingham County, settled mainly by German immigrants, is known for its

---

Two Great Ways to Enjoy the Blue Ridge

Harrisonburg/ Rockingham County & Courtyard by Marriott

Bike or camp our forests, hike or drive our parks, canoe or fish our rivers, and play golf at any one of our many courses. Minutes off the Skyline Drive, the "Friendly City" offers a vibrant downtown situated around the famous Court Square. Visit the Virginia Quilt Museum, The Court Square Theater, Endless Caverns, and Massanutten Four Seasons Resort. Shop, dine and let us entertain you in Rockingham County.

Traveler info:
Exit: MP 65
Open: Daily 9am-5pm
For more info:
Harrisonburg – Rockingham Convention & Visitors Bureau
10 E. Gay St.
Harrisonburg, VA 22802
(540) 434-2319
hrcvb@planetcomm.net
www.hrcvb.org

North Fork of the Shenandoah River with Blue Ridge Mountains in background.

Ideally located off I-81 and only blocks from James Madison University, the Courtyard is within

The Courtyard by Marriott is just minutes away from area attractions.

walking distance to shopping and restaurants. The hotel features an indoor pool, hot tub, exercise room, restaurant and complimentary high speed internet access.

Traveler info:
Exit: MP 65
Open: Daily, 24 hrs.
For more info:
Courtyard by Marriott
1890 Evelyn Byrd Ave.
Harrisonburg, VA 22801
(540) 432-3031
www.marriott.com/shdcy

❽ A ❽ B *Please refer to map*

Woodrow Wilson Museum houses exhibits telling about the life of the 28th president of the United States, including Wilson's 1919 Pierce-Arrow limousine.

A rt is an intrinsic part of Waynesboro, home to **P. Buckley Moss Museum**, the **Shenandoah Valley Art Center** and the **Artisans Center of Virginia**, where juried artworks are on display. The **Wildlife Center of Virginia** here is a hospital for wild creatures of the area. The **Waynesboro Heritage Museum** presents the Revolutionary and Civil War history of this 200-year-old town. See boxes on pages 28 and 29 for more information.

Mennonite communities. Shop the **Dayton Farmers' Market** and you'll catch sight of their buggies traveling between farms. Visit 18th-century **Fort Harrison** and the **Shenandoah Valley Heritage & Culture Center** or head to **Harrisonburg** to visit **Virginia Quilt Museum** and enjoy a concert at **Court Square Theater**. See page 27 for more information.

Waynesboro ⑩

Greater Augusta Regional Chamber of Commerce
732 Tinkling Spring Rd.
P.O. Box 1107
Fishersville, VA 22939
(540) 949-8203
(540) 324-1133
info@augustachamber.org
www.augustachamber.org
•I-64 and U.S. 250 intersect the terminus of the Skyline Drive and MP 0 of the parkway at Rockfish Gap

Staunton ⑪

Staunton Convention and Visitors Bureau
116 W. Beverley St.
Staunton, VA 24401
(540) 332-3972, (800) 332-5219
www.staunton.va.us
•From MP 0 take U.S. 250 west from Rockfish Gap

T ry a guided or self-guided tour through the five national historic districts of **Staunton** – there's

Waynesboro, Virginia

A Place for All Seasons

W aynesboro is in the beautiful Shenandoah Valley where the Blue Ridge Parkway and Skyline Drive meet. Enjoy hiking, camping, skiing, cycling, golf and the natural beauty of our mountains. Experience the Virginia Fall Foliage Festival and Art Show, Artisan Center of Virginia, local antique shops and the P.

Fly-fishing is one of the many outdoor recreational activities available in Waynesboro.

Our many festivals highlight Waynesboro's sense of family and community.

Buckley Moss Museum. Canoe, fish or kayak our South River. Explore our Main Street and historic districts, Civil War sites, unique shops, fine dining and accommodations.

Traveler info:
Distance: Approx. 3 miles from Parkway
Event Calendar: April 16-17 – Fly Fishing Festival; April 23 – Riverfest; May 21 – Blue Ridge Soap Box Classic;

July 9-10 – Summer Extravaganza; Oct. 1-2 and 9-10 – Fall Foliage Festival; Oct. 8-9– Virginia Fall Foliage Festival Art Show; Dec. 31 – First Night Waynesboro
For more info:
Office of Tourism
PO Box 1028
Waynesboro, VA 22980
(866) 253-1957
crookshanksll@ci.waynesboro.va.us
www.waynesboro.va.us

⑩ *Please refer to map*

PAT & CHUCK BLACKLEY

A woman makes buttermilk in Staunton's Frontier Culture Museum.

even a trolley. Long a railroad town, Staunton is the only town in the Shenandoah Valley with a passenger station. Sights to see include **Woodrow Wilson Birthplace & Museum, Statler Brothers Museum & Complex** and **Andre Viette Gardens** at Fishersville.

Frontier Culture Museum ⑪A

1290 Richmond Rd.
Staunton, VA 24401
(540) 332-7850
info@frontiermuseum.state.va.us
www.frontiermuseum.org
•Approximately 15 miles from MP 0

Experience life in four countries in three centuries – in just a few hours at the Frontier Culture Museum. The international living-history museum features four historic farms (German, Scotch-Irish, American, English) of pre-immigration Europe and pre-Civil War Virginia. Costumed interpreters demonstrate farming, cooking, blacksmithing and other skills necessary to life on these farms. Also see page 29 box.

Lexington ⑫

Lexington & the Rockbridge Area Visitor Center
106 E. Washington St.
Lexington, VA 24450
(540) 463-3777
(877) 4LEXVA2

Frontier Culture Museum

Visit Old-World Germany, England, Northern Ireland, and 19th Century America

Experience four countries set in three centuries...in just a few hours at the Frontier Culture Museum in the Shenandoah Valley! This international living history museum features four historic farms of pre-immigration Europe and pre-Civil War Virginia. Costumed staff demonstrate trades and traditions through agriculture, blacksmithing, gardens, cooking, and household programs. Rare and minor breed livestock live at each farm.

Visit a Scotch-Irish farm, circa 1730.

Traveler info:
Distance: Approx. 15 miles from Parkway MP 0
Open: 9am-5pm (mid-March-Nov.); 10am-4pm (Dec.-mid-March). Closed Thanksgiving, Christmas, and New Year's.
♿

For more info:
Frontier Culture Museum
P.O. Box 810
Staunton, VA 24401
(540) 332-7850
info@fcmv.virginia.gov
www.frontier.virginia.gov

⑪ A *Please refer to map*

The P. Buckley Moss Museum

A Permanent Exhibition of the Art of Virginia's Own P. Buckley Moss

The P. Buckley Moss Museum, located in the heart of the Shenandoah Valley in Waynesboro, Virginia, exhibits works by P. Buckley Moss, one of America's most recognized and most popular artists. Moss has found her inspiration and much of her subject matter in Valley scenery and in the Amish and Mennonite peoples of the area. Free admission. Guided tours.

Handcrafted With Love

Traveler info:
Exit: MP 0
Open: Mon.-Sat. 10am-6pm; Sun. 12:30pm-5:30pm
Admission: Free
For more info:
P. Buckley Moss Museum
150 P. Buckley Moss Dr.
Waynesboro, VA 22980
(540) 949-6473
www.pbuckleymoss.com

⑩ A *Please refer to map*

Natural Bridge

Explore a Beautiful Nature Park and a National Historic Landmark

Visit one of the nation's most recognized wonders of nature.

Come face to face with nature's remarkable power, the Natural Bridge. Then meet members of the Monacan Indian Nation; journey back 300 years with interpreters at the Monacan Indian Living History Village. Stroll to Lace Waterfalls. Relax at the Summerhouse Cafe before descending into the striking underground world of Natural Bridge Caverns. Re-surface and visit The Toy Museum at Natural Bridge, The Natural Bridge Wax Museum and The Haunted Monster Museum. Have dinner and stay at our full-service hotel.

Traveler info:
Exit: MP 45.6, 61.6, 63.7
Open: 8am till sunset
Admission: $10 adults, $5 children ages 5-12
For more info:
Natural Bridge of Virginia
US 11 & VA 130
Natural Bridge, VA 24578
(800) 533-1410
info@naturalbridgeva.com
www.naturalbridgeva.com

13 *Please refer to map*

Virginia's Explore Park

A Delightful Stroll Through History

Blacksmithing is one of many skills demonstrated at Virginia's Explore Park.

While enjoying a leisurely stroll through the forest, experience first hand the life of the 1671 Native American, the rugged existence of the 1757 frontier fort dweller and the evolution of an 1850's community in young America. Year-round, visitors can savor lunch or dinner, served Wednesday through Sunday, at the Historic Brugh Tavern, or enjoy mountain biking, hiking, fishing and picnicking from dawn to dusk daily at no charge.

Open: Historic Areas Wed-Sat. 10am-5pm; Sun. Noon-5pm; Apr. (weekends)-Oct.
Admission: General $8; Seniors (55+) $6; Youth (4-15) $5; three and under free.
For more info:
Virginia's Explore Park
PO Box 8508
Roanoke, VA 24014
(540) 427-1800
www.explorepark.org

Traveler info:
Exit: MP 115

15 *Please refer to map*

---

www.lexingtonvirginia.com
•3 access points in Rockbridge County: MP 27, 45.6 and 63.7
•144 Confederate soldiers are buried in Stonewall Jackson Memorial Cemetery

Washington and Lee University and Virginia Military Institute are located in **Lexington**. The town was once home and current resting place of Robert E. Lee and Stonewall Jackson. The **Lee Chapel and Museum**, holding the tombs of Lee, his family and his horse; **Stonewall Jackson House**, the only house Jack-

COURTESY LEXINGTON & ROCKBRIDGE AREA

Stonewall Jackson's statue stands in front of the barracks at VMI.

Stonewall Jackson

The only home Confederate General Thomas Jonathan "Stonewall" Jackson ever owned is in Lexington, and this is where he is buried.

After teaching at VMI for 10 years he joined the Confederate army as General Robert E. Lee's right hand with orders to defend the Shenandoah Valley. The valley was important to the strategies of both sides during the Civil War, it was a fertile breadbasket and also could allow troops to march almost unseen to Washington D.C. or Richmond. In Jackson's two-year Valley Campaign he used speed, surprise and his knowledge of the area topography to defend the valley against Union troops that far outnumbered his.

Standing firm at the First Battle of Bull Run earned Jackson his nickname, Stonewall.

son ever owned; and **George C. Marshall Museum** are historic stops. **Lime Kiln Theatre** hosts outdoor concerts and plays. **Virginia Horse Center** is the site of horse shows year-round.

Natural Bridge/ Natural Chimneys

Natural Bridge **⑬**
US 11 & VA 130
Natural Bridge, VA 24578
(800) 533-1410
info@naturalbridgeva.com
www.naturalbridgeva.com
•Take Va. 130 from MP 61.6 or U.S. 501 from MP 63.9

Natural Chimneys Regional **⑨**
Park
Mt. Solon, VA 24578
(540) 350-2510
www.uvrpa.org
•Take U.S. 33 west at Skyline Drive MP 65.5 to U.S. 42 south to Va. 731

Natural Bridge, "one of the seven wonders of the world," was once owned by Thomas Jefferson. U.S. 11 actually passes over the 215-

COURTESY VIRGINIA TOURISM CORPORATION

Formed when ancient oceans disappeared, Mt. Solon's Natural Chimneys are left, and every year it is the site of jousting tournaments.

foot-high bridge. An inn, zoo, caverns and wax museum are also located at the site.

Natural Chimneys, formed by an ancient sea that once filled the valley, is now a regional park with campground plus hiking/ biking trails. Since 1821, Natural Chimneys has held an annual jousting tournament. See box on facing page for more information.

Roanoke **⑭**

Roanoke Valley Convention & Visitors Bureau
101 Shenandoah Avenue NE
Roanoke, VA 24016
(540) 342-6025, (800) 635-5535
info@visitroanokeva.com
www.visitroanokeva.com
•Three points of departure from the Parkway: U.S. 460/221, Va. 24 and U.S. 220, all between MP 105 and MP 125
•An entire mountain sits within the borders of this city of 100,000

The Capital of the Blue Ridge

Discover Virginia's Roanoke Valley, Virginia's Largest Metropolitan Destination on the Blue Ridge Parkway

Located at MP 120, the mountain views are only the beginning of what you will find in the area. Experience the perfect blend of mountain sites and city lights. Whether it is cultural

The view of the Roanoke Valley from the Roanoke Star.

Roanoke offers the best of both worlds, a unique blend of urban and rural environments.

experiences or living history, spectator or participatory sports, farmers' markets and the largest number of restaurants per capita in the Commonwealth, you'll find something to enjoy in the Roanoke Valley. Experience festivals, family fun, antiques, and art galleries. With over 6,000 first-class guestrooms, you can renew yourself for another day of excitement at a cozy bed and breakfast or a state-of-the-art-hotel. The Roanoke

Valley has many attributes to charm any visitor...it's in our nature! Free visitors guide or golf package information.

Traveler info:
Exit: MP 120
Open: Varies seasonally
For more info:
Roanoke Valley Convention and Visitors Bureau
101 Shenandoah Ave., NE
Roanoke, VA 24016
(800) 635-5535
www.VisitRoanokeVA.com

⑭ A ⑭ C *Please refer to map*

A woman spins at Virginia's Explore Park, MP 115 near Roanoke.

PAT & CHUCK BLACKLEY

Museum of African American Culture.

The famous 100-foot-high **Roanoke Star** atop **Mill Mountain** is the symbol of the "Star City." **Mill Mountain Zoo** is open year-round. See page 31 for more information

Virginia's Explore Park ⑮

The Norfolk & Western J-class locomotives were built from 1941 to 1950. The 611 is now housed at the Virginia Museum of Transportation in Roanoke.

JIM W

Downtown Roanoke is home to the year-round farmers' market plus shops and fine restaurants. **Center in the Square** houses the city's regional theater, science museum, history museum and art museum. The city's railroad ties are seen at **Hotel Roanoke** and the **Virginia Museum of Transportation** as well as the newly opened **O. Winston Link Museum.** Nearby is the **Harrison**

3900 Rutrough Rd.
P.O. Box 8508
Roanoke, VA 24014-0508
(540) 427-1800
(800) 842-9163
www.explorepark.org
•Roanoke River Parkway spur at MP 115 near Roanoke

History and recreation abound at Explore Park. Travel forest footpaths to the 1671 Totero Village, 1740 Settler's Cabin and 19th Century Valley Community with costumed interpreters to greet you. Brugh Tavern, c. 1800s, is open seasonally for dining.

Many workshops and events are held including Appalachian Heritage Festival in September.

Roanoke River bisects the park; canoeing, kayaking and fishing are popular. More than 10 miles of bike trails wind through the area. For more information see page 30.

Historic Hotel Roanoke

Enjoy Traditional Southern Hospitality

Nestled in the heart of the Blue Ridge Mountains, The Hotel Roanoke & Conference Center surrounds you with the warmest of traditional southern hospitality. Since 1882, the Hotel Roanoke has charmed everyone from Presidents to beauty queens, plus countless residents and visitors. The magnificent half-timber Tudor

Historic Hotel Roanoke in downtown Roanoke.

Revival building, listed on the National Historic Register, is a centerpiece of the city's rich heritage and has been restored to its rich, 19th-century elegance. Savor elegant fare in the award-winning Regency Dining Room. Relax in the casual Pine Room Pub. Or wind-down in the outdoor swimming pool, whirlpool and fitness center, with golf and tennis nearby. Experience the history and charm of the city through our dramatic Market Square

Bridge, where galleries, shopping, entertainment and museums await you.

Traveler info:
Distance: 5 miles from Parkway
Rates: $84-$450 suites
For more info:
Hotel Roanoke
110 Shenandoah Ave.
Roanoke, VA 24016
(800) 222-TREE
(540) 985-5900
www.hotelroanoke.com

The Hotel Roanoke offers luxurious accommodations.

14 B *Please refer to map*

The Valley's Caverns

Visit the Shenandoah Valley Travel Association's website for individual links: www.svta.org.

⑯Crystal Caverns at Hupp's Hill, Strasburg. History tied to the Civil War, located with the Stonewall Jackson Museum and site of several battles. (540) 465-5884.

⑰Dixie Caverns, Salem. Discovered by farm boys in 1920, the caverns property now offers camping, antiques and pottery. (540) 380-2085.

❻ₐEndless Caverns, New Market. Located in historic New Market, there is a wooded campground, open all year. (800) 544-CAVE.

⑱Grand Caverns, Grottoes. Grottoes highlight both geological and Civil War history. Rated #2 caverns in U.S. by *Parade Magazine*. (888) 430-CAVE.

⑲Luray Caverns, Luray. Features singing tower and stalacpipe organ. (540) 743-6551.

⑳Shenandoah Caverns. Only cavern with an elevator, collection of parade floats. (888) 4CAVERNS.

㉑Skyline Caverns, Front Royal. Located in Warren County, it features beautiful and rare anthodites "orchids of the mineral kingdom." (800) 296-4545.

COURTESY VIRGINIA TOURISM CORPORATION

Luray Caverns' dramatic beauty is typical of the caves of the region. This formation is one of the most perfectly formed drapery structures in the world.

SHENANDOAH VALLEY SERVICES

DOWNTOWN ROANOKE CITY MARKET

MP 121.4 • 213 Market St. • Roanoke, VA 24011 • (540) 342-2028 • Open year-round Mon.-Sat.

History, tradition, friendly faces and timeless beauty in one lively place. Celebrating 120 years, Roanoke's Market is the place to browse and enjoy fresh vegetables, fruits, flowers, plants, and a huge variety of artisan crafts in an area surrounded by eclectic shops, dining options, museums and art galleries.

www.downtownroanoke.org

www.grandcaverns.com

GRAND CAVERNS

5 Caverns Dr. • Grottoes, VA 24441 • (888) 430-CAVE • Open: Daily Apr.-Oct., weekends only, Nov.-Mar., 9am-5pm.

Hear the echoes of history and explore the beauty that continues to unfold under the surface of the earth in one of Virginia's spectacular caverns. Offering tours since 1806, Grand Caverns recently received the second highest ranking of "show caves" in the US by Parade magazine.

SLEEP INN ROANOKE

Distance: Approx. 2 miles from Parkway • 4045 Electric Rd. • Roanoke, VA 24014 • (540) 772-1500 • Rates: $39-$99 • Rooms: 81 • AE, V, MC, DC

The Newly Remodeled Sleep Inn at Tanglewood is the perfect place to enjoy what Roanoke has to offer after a your scenic drive on the Parkway. Easy access to and from the parkway. Located two miles off the parkway at milepost 121.

www.dominionlodging.com

Virginia's Jefferson Country

Skyline Drive MP 80 to Parkway MP 116
Orange County • Charlottesville • Nelson County • Lynchburg • Bedford • Smith Mountain Lake

I f Virginia is the mother of presidents, then this part of the state is the cradle. The legacies of Jefferson, Monroe and Madison are alive here, as are Virginia's venerable wine history, her ties to the Civil War and some of her most stunning outdoor spots.

Tour Virginia's Jefferson Country and witness the genius of Thomas Jefferson at many turns in the road. From his unique architectural details at Monticello to his octagonal personal masterpiece, Poplar Forest and the awe-inspiring rotunda at the University of Virginia, Jefferson's ideas, innovations and institutions abound here.

Visit Bedford and remember the sacrifice this small city and surrounding county made on D-Day. Save time for hiking the Peaks of Otter or shushing down the slopes at Wintergreen Resort. Visit beautiful Smith Mountain Lake and boat along its 500 miles of shoreline.

Charlottesville and Lynchburg are the region's primary cities, offering urban amenities with a small-town feel.

And this is the region where the Skyline Drive and the Blue Ridge Parkway meet in their collective excursion along the spine of the Virginia Blue Ridge.

JIM WAITE

The weekly Fridays After Five festivities take place on the downtown pedestrian mall in Charlottesville.

◁ *Monticello, the home of Thomas Jefferson, is a highlight of a Charlottesville visit.*

JIM WAITE

Spy Rock, a 3.2-mile hike away from Parkway MP 27.2, offers one of the most spectacular views in the region.

Getting Around

The Skyline Drive and Blue Ridge Parkway meet in Jefferson Country, at Rockfish Gap near Waynesboro. Their pretty miles are paralleled by equally scenic stretches of the famed Appalachian Trail, which spends more than 500 of its 2,100+ miles (from Maine to Georgia) in Virginia. Also paralleling are the primary north-south routes of the region: Interstate 81 and old U.S. 11 to the west and U.S. 29 to the east. The major east-west roadways are I-64 (paralleled by U.S. 250) across the northern part of the region, U.S. 60 and 501 across the central area, and U.S. 460 and 221 (which then turns south to parallel the Parkway) across the southern area.

KEY

▬	Blue Ridge Parkway
▬	Skyline Drive
▬	Highways
—	Secondary Roads
▬	Rivers/Lakes
▲	Overlooks
⌣	Tunnels
MP	Mileposts
⛽	Gasoline
⚦	Restrooms
∭	Food
⼍	Picnicking
♣	Visitor Center
♣	State Park

TED PRATT

Smith Mountain Lake is a haven for boaters who like speed, and also those who like sails.

• Between 1818 and 1820, Thomas Jefferson Beale is supposed to have buried 3,000 pounds of gold and 5,000 pounds of silver along with thousands of dollars in jewels. He left three numerical ciphers describing the location of the cache in Bedford County. Many have tried breaking the codes and many have dug for it, but it remains hidden to this day.

Map labels: N   Shenandoah   MP 5.8   2   6   151   MP 29   5   56   6   4   60   MP 60.9   MP 63.8   MP 86   501   Lynchburg   James River   9   43   7   221   460   Appomattox   8   Bedford   10   460   24   Smith Mountain Lake State Park   Smith Mountain Lake   11

More Rain Than Ever – Anywhere

The night of August 19-20, 1969 in Nelson County, Va. unveiled one of the most astounding outbursts of weather on earth. Up to 46 inches of rain poured out of the sky in a once-in-10,000-years inland meteorological occurrence that unleashed a power equal to a 40,000-megaton nuclear bomb. About 630 million tons of water fell on the county's 471 square miles, taking 111 lives. Annual rainfall on the Parkway averages in the 40-inch range.

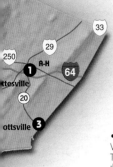

JIM WAITE

•Charlottesville's University of Virginia campus, designed by Thomas Jefferson, was voted the most outstanding achievement in American architecture by the American Institute of Architects in 1976.

10 miles

Moses Ezekiel's statue of Thomas Jefferson stands in front of Jefferson's Rotunda at the head of UVa's Lawn, one of America's architectural masterpieces.

Holliday Lake State Park

SIGHTS AND SITES AT A GLANCE

❶ Charlottesville
   ❶ A Ash Lawn-Highland
   ❶ B Charlottesville Area Golf Courses
   ❶ C Charlottesville Art Galleries
   ❶ D Historic District of Charlottesville
   ❶ E Michie Tavern
   ❶ F Monticello
   ❶ G University of Virginia Rotunda and Central Grounds
   ❶ H Monticello Region Wineries

❷ Afton
❸ James River
❹ Nelson County
❺ Wintergreen
❻ Lovingston
❼ Lynchburg
   ❼ A Lynchburg Visitor Center
   ❼ B Historic Districts
   ❼ C Old City Cemetery
❽ Appomatox Courthouse
❾ Peaks of Otter

❿ Bedford
   ❿ A Thomas Jefferson's Poplar Forest
   ❿ B National D-Day Memorial
   ❿ C Orchards & Wineries
⓫ Smith Mountain Lake

See also:
   Traveler Services p. 47;
   Trip Planner Listings p. 130

🌳 For specific locations of state parks see www.dcr.state.va.us/parks or call (800) 933-PARK.

Monticello ➊F

Va. 53 (Thomas Jefferson Pkwy.)
PO Box 316
Charlottesville, VA 22902
(434) 984-9800
(434) 984-9822
www.monticello.org
•MP 0, take I-64 east to Va. 20
south to Va. 53, 3 miles southeast of Charlottesville
•Jefferson died here on July 4,
1826, the 50th anniversary of
the Declaration of Independence

The Garden Pavilion was among Jeffersons favorite places to sit, read and look out over the garden and mountains beyond.

Monticello is the home of Thomas Jefferson, third U.S. President, author and founder of the University of Virginia. In 1769 at the age of 26, Thomas Jefferson began the design and construction of Monticello. Perched on a mountaintop overlooking the City of Charlottesville, Monticello is a majestic reminder of Jefferson's creativity and talent. The house was built and subsequently remodeled over a period of 40 years.

The home is owned and operated by the Thomas Jefferson Memorial Foundation, which has continued to restore the house and create an authentic Jeffersonian atmosphere. The house currently contains many original family furnishings. On the grounds, Jefferson's interest in horticulture has come alive with the painstaking re-creation of his orchard, vineyard and vegetable garden. Guided tours of the home are available daily, and visitors are encouraged to wander through the magnificent gardens, which surround the home.

Historic District of Charlottesville ➊D

Charlottesville, VA
(877) 386-1102
•MP 0, take I-64 east to U.S. 29 north

Listed on the National Register of Historic Places, the historic district includes taverns and shops around Court Square, an area frequented by Jefferson, Madison and Monroe. The Albemarle County Historical Society, (434) 296-1492, offers walking tours of the district by appointment.

For visitors and local residents alike, the Historic District is also a magnet for art, music, dining, shopping

The pedestrian mall in Charlottesville's historic district is a charming place to spend an afternoon, with shopping, great restaurants and good entertainment.

and entertainment. Along its pedestrian mall, strollers enjoy numerous galleries, antique stores, booksellers and locally owned restaurants and eateries. See box on page 41 for more information.

Charlottesville Art Galleries ➊C

University of Virginia Art Museum, Rugby Road, Charlottesville
(434) 924-3592, www.virginia.edu/artmuseum.
Kluge-Ruhe Aboriginal Art Collection of the University of Virginia, 400 Worrell Dr., Peter Jefferson Place, Charlottesville.
(434) 244-0234. www.virginia.edu/kluge-ruhe.
McGuffey Art Center, 201 Second St. NW, Charlottesville.
(434) 295-7973.
www.mcguffeyartcenter.com.
Second Street Gallery, 201 Second St. NW, Charlottesville.
(434) 977-7284
www.secondstreet-gallery.org

Charlottesville Area Golf Courses ➊B

Birdwood at the Boar's Head Inn, 18 holes, par 72. U.S. 250 West, Charlottesville. (434) 293-GOLF.
Keswick Hall at Monticello, 18 holes par 71, 701 Club Dr., Keswick.
(434) 979-3440.
Meadow Creek Golf

Course, City of Charlottesville, 18 holes, par 71, Pen Park Rd., Charlottesville, (434) 977-0615.

Swannanoa Country Club, 18 holes, par 70, Va. 610, Afton. (540) 943-8864.

University of Virginia Rotunda & Central Grounds ❶G

University Information Center, Ivy Road, (US 250 Business) Charlottesville, VA 22902 (434) 924-0311
www.virginia.edu
•MP 0, take I-64 east to U.S. 29 bypass to U.S. 250 east to 29 Business

It is said that Thomas Jefferson wanted to be remembered as the "Father" of the University of Virginia. Long a champion of democracy and education, Jefferson founded the University of Virginia in an effort to provide education to everyone "regardless of wealth, birth or other accidental condition or circumstance." Free guided tours are available of Jefferson's architectural achievements here. Tour Jefferson's "academical" village of 10 pavilions, the University's rotunda with its flowing hourglass shape, the Lawn and the Pavilion Gardens which include many plants grown at Monticello.

The view of the James River from the parkway bridge at MP 63.6 has been compared to "the mountain-set beauty of the Rhine."

PAT & CHUCK BLACKLEY

Ash Lawn-Highland ❶A

1000 James Monroe Parkway Charlottesville, VA 22902 (434) 293-9539
www.ashlawnhighland.org
•MP 0, take I-64 east to Va. 20 south to Va. 53 to Va. 795, 2.5 miles from Monticello

Ash Lawn-Highland, home of the fifth president of the United States James Monroe, is owned/operated by the College of William and Mary, Monroe's alma mater. The 550-acre estate features a working farm, house and garden tours plus 19th century cooking demonstrations. The Ashlawn Opera Festival is held each summer in the estate gardens.

Michie Tavern ❶E

683 Thomas Jefferson Parkway Charlottesville, VA 22902 (434) 977-1234 info@michietavern.com
www.michietavern.com
•MP 0, take I-64 east to Va. 20 south to Va. 53 (1/2 mile from Monticello)

Ca. 1784, Michie Tavern has welcomed travelers for more than 200 years. Today, visitors may dine on "homemade southern fare" and then tour the inn accompanied by 18th-century costumed interpreters.

The Virginia Wine Museum is located in the Tavern's wine cellar. Gifts are offered at the General Store, Museum Shop and recently added Printer's Shop.

The James River ❸

• **Hatton Ferry.** The Hatton Ferry, one of only two poled ferries still operating in the United States, runs April 15 through October 15 on Fridays, Saturdays and Sundays, and visitors may ride across the river at no charge if water levels permit. The ferry is outside Scottsville on Va. 625. (434) 296-1492.
www.hattonferry.org
• Day or overnight on the James River. Equipment and transportation provided. Canoeing, rafting or tubing. **James River Reeling and Rafting**, Scottsville (434) 286-4386, www.ReelingandRafting.com. **James River Runners**, Scottsville (434) 286-2338, www.jamesriver.com. Historic downtown Scottsville has two new walking parks and a museum offering a history of the river.

PAT & CHUCK BLACKLEY

Charlottesville's Michie Tavern offers sumptuous meals.

Crabtree Falls has been listed as a 1,200-foot drop; it's actually five falls with smaller, connecting cascades.

CHARLES SHOFFNER

Devil's Knob at Wintergreen. Nelson County. (434) 325-8240. Newly redesigned, this course at 3,850 feet is the highest in Virginia. 18 holes, par 70. Open April-October.

Stoney Creek at Wintergreen. Nelson County. (434) 325-8250, 27 holes, par 72. Open year-round, Rees Jones designed, rated #34 best resort course in U.S. by *Golf Digest*.

Appomattox Courthouse ❽

Appomattox Court House
National Historical Park
Va. 24, PO Box 218
Appomattox, VA 24522
(434) 352-8987 x 26
www.nps.gov/apco
•MP 63.8 U.S. 501, U.S. 460

Visit the place where General Robert E. Lee of the Army of Northern Virginia, surrendered to General Ulysses Grant, on April 9, 1865, ending the Civil War. The National Park encompasses approximately 1,800 acres and includes the McLean home (surrender site) and the village of Appomattox Court House. The site also has the home and burial place of Joel Sweeney – the popularizer of the modern five string banjo. There are 27 original 19th century structures on the site.

Nelson County ❹

P.O. Box 636
Lovingston, VA 22949
(800) 282-8223
www.nelsoncounty.com
•MP 13.5, take Va. 664; MP 16, take Va. 814; MP 27.2, take Va. 56
•Crabtree Falls is the highest cascading waterfall east of the Mississippi River

Skiing, hiking, wine-tasting and history combine in Nelson County. Towering **Crabtree Falls**, with five cascades totaling 1,200 feet, has hiking trails and cabins (Cabins at Crabtree Falls: www.crabtreefalls.com). **Walton's Mountain Museum** at Schuyler is popular with those who loved the TV series, www.waltonmuseum.org.

   Wintergreen Resort, Va. 664 at Wintergreen, is a top destination for skiers and golfers and it is home to Wintergreen Nature Foundation, which hosts workshops and hikes year-round. Six wineries and orchards offer special events.

Wintergreen Resort Golf Courses ❺

Box 706
Wintergreen, VA 22958
www.wintergreenresort.com
•MP 135, take VA 664

Jefferson's Poplar Forest, where the nation's third president sought solitude, is open for tours as restoration continues; the goal is to return the octagonal home to its appearance when Jefferson lived there.

Charlottesville/Albemarle County

So Very Virginia!

Only thirty minutes from the Blue Ridge Parkway, this micropolitan city offers the best of the South, with a dynamic town center, elegant architecture, museums and recreational activities to tempt visitors all year round.

Three presidents made their homes here. The influence of Thomas Jefferson is everywhere, from his mountaintop home, Monticello, to his beloved University of Virginia, which he founded and considered his crowning achievement. Tours of Monticello's magnificent interior and fabulous gardens are available daily, as are tours of Montpelier, home of James and Dolley Madison and Ash Lawn-Highland, the home of President James Monroe, who negotiated the Lousiana Purchase.

Other nearby attractions include Michie Tavern ca.1784, offering tours and a hearty colonial southern lunch, the quaint town of Scottsville, nestled next to the James River, and the Monticello Wine

Shopping, entertainment and dining opportunities are plentiful on the Downtown Mall.

Trail, a collection of seventeen area award-winning wineries, whose tours, tastings and special events

King Family Vineyard is the winner of the 2004 Virginia Governor's Cup.

delight visitors throughout the year.

For those who love the outdoors, activities are plentiful, with mountain biking, hiking, rock climbing, ballooning and camping. The James River provides kayaking, rafting, tubing and fishing- or enjoy a unique river crossing at Hatton's Ferry, one of only two poled ferries operating in the country.

Complete your visit with a tour of the historic downtown pedestrian mall and Court Square. Live the best of small town America as you enjoy concerts and museums or visit restaurants, galleries, theaters, coffee houses and specialty shops that let you bring home a little bit of your stay.

Find out why Charlottesville and Albemarle County are So Very Virginia!

Traveler info:
Distance: 20 miles from Parkway
For more info:
Charlottesville/Albemarle Convention and Visitors Bureau
PO Box 178
Charlottesville, VA 22902
(877) 386-1102
www.SoVeryVirginia.com

See Thomas Jefferson's masterpiece, the Rotunda on the grounds of the University of Virginia.

 1 A   **1** B   **1** C   *Please refer to map*

Abbott Lake, at the Peaks of Otter at MP 86, honors the parkway's first landscape architect, Stanley Abbott.

Lynchburg ❼

Lynchburg Regional Convention
& Visitors Bureau
Corner of 12th & Church Streets
(800) 732-5821
(434) 847-1811
tourism@lynchburgchamber.org
www.discoverlynchburg.org
•MP 63.8, U.S. 501

Tour Lynchburg's five historic districts of more than 240 buildings. Nearby is **Lynchburg Museum at the Old Court House** and **Amazement Square-Rightmire Children's Museum**.

The Old City Cemetery & Arboretum is a 200-year old historic landmark with four small museums and a confederate section (434) 847-1465. Nearby is the **Legacy Museum of African-American History**, (434) 845-3455. **Point of Honor** is the 1815 Federal-style mansion of Patrick Henry's friend and physician Dr. George Cabell, Sr. (434) 847-1459. For more information see box on page 43.

Jefferson's Poplar Forest ❿ₐ

P.O. Box 419
Forest, VA 24551-0419
(434) 525-1806
www.poplarforest.org
•MP 86, Va. 43 to Va. 661

Calling it "the most valuable of my possessions," Thomas Jefferson enjoyed this year-round retreat near Lynchburg. On a 4,800-acre plantation in Bedford County, Jefferson built his "dream house" – an octagonal house surrounded by a villa landscape. Rescue of the house began in 1984; visitors can watch the restoration that is still under way today.

Peaks of Otter Area & Lodge ❾

PO Box 489
Bedford, VA 24523
(540) 586-1081
(800) 542-5927
peaksotter@aol.com
www.peaksofotter.com
•MP 86

Hike the three Peaks of Otter with **Peaks of Otter Lodge and Restaurant** as your home base. Hike Flat Top,

4,001 feet or Harkening Hill, 3,375 feet (each a 1.5- to 2-mile walk). Hike or ride the bus to the summit of Sharp Top, 3,865 feet for a 360-degree view.

Hike to the historic Johnson Farm.

The lodge overlooks Abbott Lake; the full-service restaurant includes a wine list.

Bedford ❿

Bedford Area Visitors Center
816 Burks Hill Rd.
Bedford, VA 24523
(540) 586-9401
(800) 933-9535
(877) HI-PEAKS
info@bedfordareachamber.com
www.bedfordareachamber.com
www.visitbedford.com
•MP 86, VA 43 or MP 105.8, US 460
•Bedford lost 21 sons at continued or page 47

December 6, 1944 is remembered at the National D-Day Memorial in Bedford.

Discover Lynchburg ... In Every Direction

History, Natural Beauty, Arts and Culture in Every Direction

Lynchburg is known as the Hill City. On some of these hills rest beautiful Historic Districts, which offer a panoramic view of the historic James River and the Blue Ridge mountains. Tour Lynchburg's six nationally recognized Historic Districts by car or by foot. Over 240 properties are included in a Historic District Tour brochure available at the Lynchburg Visitors Center.

If you enjoy architecture, Lynchburg is a genuine find with many diverse styles of the 18th, 19th and early 20th centuries.

Point of Honor, one of Virginia's most remarkable Federal-style mansions, is located on Daniels Hill. The Old Court House, built in 1855, is an excellent example of Greek Revival architecture, and is located on Court House Hill atop Monument

Blackwater Creek Trail.

Terrace. The Legacy Museum of African-American History is located in a charming Victorian home next to Old City Cemetery - a 200 year-old Virginia Historic Landmark.

Housed in a newly restored circa 1862 warehouse overlooking the James River is Amazement Square, The Rightmire Children's Museum.

The Rightmire Children's Museum offers more than 29,000 square feet of hands on activities for children.

Blackwater Creek Bikeway & Riverwalk meanders through the city of Lynchburg with eight miles of trails. Near the center of the 300-acre

Monument Terrace is a decorative stairway leading to the Old Court House.

Natural area is the 155-acre Ruskin Freer Nature Preserve, a plant and animal sanctuary.

Plan to spend the night. Many attractions are within an hours drive and more than 1,800 rooms ranging from elegant bed and breakfast inns to luxury hotels are available.

Traveler info:
Distance: 20 miles from Parkway
&

For more info:
Lynchburg Regional Convention and Visitors Bureau
216 Twelfth St.
Lynchburg, VA 24504
(800) 732-5821
(434) 847-1811
Tourism@LynchburgChamber.org
www.DiscoverLynchburg.org

Discover the diverse architecture in Lynchburg.

7 A   **7** B   **7** C   *Please refer to map*

New Welcome Center A "Must See"

An Attraction in Itself

This Fall Bedford City and County opened their state-of-the-art Welcome Center, conceived to serve both visitors and citizens as a resource for area, statewide, Mid-Atlantic, special event and travel information as well as a community meeting and event center. With its extensive library of brochures and information, the assistance of the travel counselors, internet stations and wireless connections, travel and tourism related questions are handled quickly and efficiently.

The Welcome Center sits on a 2.4 acre site at the intersection of Rt. 122 and U.S. 460, adjacent to The National D-Day Memorial.

The Center's interior amenities include a gift shop, attraction and lodging exhibits, interactive computer kiosk, Travel Gallery, Firefighters Gallery, a coffee bar, internet stations and theatre.

The remaining two galleries contain tourism offices, a beverage & snack area and a large community room that may be used for receptions, seminars or meetings. Exterior amenities include a large terrace,

Located right below The National D-Day Memorial, Bedford's new Welcome Center serves as a gateway to the region and offers travelers a relaxing setting amidst awe-inspiring views.

Knowledgeable travel counselors assist all visitors with a warm welcome and a smile.

picnic area, dog walking area, overnight spaces with full hook ups (water, electric, sewer & wireless) for campers and RV's, motorcoach parking and unloading areas, and 1/3 mile paved walking track.

With distinctive destinations like the Parkway, the Peaks of Otter, The National D-Day Memorial, Thomas Jefferson's Poplar Forest, Smith Mountain Lake, HolyLand, plus its wineries, orchards, historical and cultural amenities, only a first-class Welcome Center could appropriately highlight these attractions. You'll want to make it your first-stop to the region.

Traveler info:
Distance: 12 miles from Parkway
Open: Daily 9am-5pm; Summer Hours: 9am-7pm
Admission: None; gift shop accepts V, MC, D
♿

For more info:
Bedford Area Welcome Center
816 Burks Hill Rd.
Bedford, VA 24523
(877) Hi Peaks (447-3257)
(540) 587-5681
nanci@visitbedford.com
www.visitbedford.com

The National D-Day Memorial memorializes and honors the tremendous sacrifices made for the cause of freedom.

 A   B   C *Please refer to map*

Explore Nelson County Virginia

The First 30 Miles of the Parkway

From the Blue Ridge Mountains to the James River - you're invited to experience adventure in our 471 square mile playground of natural beauty.

Wineries – Visit one of our seven wineries - each with award winning wines and unique, scenic settings.

Apple and Peach Orchards – More than forty varieties of apples and peaches are grown in our eight orchards - spring apple blossoms paint the mountainsides pink and white, while each fall weekend, harvest festivals celebrate nature's bounty.

Destination - The Great Outdoors - Conquer Crabtree Falls, the highest cascading waterfall east of the Mississippi River. Hike the two-mile trail for panoramic views of the valley.

Explore Nelson County's 19,411 acres of the George Washington and Jefferson National Forests, hike any of the twenty-five miles of the

Seven wineries throughout Nelson County offer tastings and specialty foods.

Hike and picnic at Crabtree Falls.

Appalachian Trail, Fortune's Cove Preserve, Blue Ridge Rail Trail or the Nelson County Wilderness Area.

Nelson County has nine watchable wildlife loops listed with the Virginia Birding and Wildlife Trail program. Fish the Tye, James and Piney Rivers, and Lake Nelson, all offering experience for all levels. With both gentle rolling hills and challenging mountain terrain, Nelson County has something for every skill level of cyclist.

Tour the Montebello State Fish Hatchery, where each year 170,000 newly hatched brook, brown and rainbow trout are nurtured to maturity, then released to stock trout waters east of the Blue Ridge Mountains.

Traveler info:
Distance: Between 1-27 miles from Parkway
For more info:
Nelson County CVB
PO Box 636
Lovingston, VA 22949
(800) 282-8223
www.nelsoncounty.com
info@nelsoncounty.org

Virginia is for Lovers

2 **5** **6**   *Please refer to map*

A scenic view from a Blue Ridge Parkway overlook.

Wine Tasting in Jefferson County

*Unique Tours
and Tastings in the
Monticello Region!*

**AFTON MOUNTAIN
VINEYARDS**
234 Vineyard Ln.
Afton, VA 22920
(540) 456-8667
www.aftonmountainvineyards.com
Open: Mar.-Oct. 10am-
6pm; Nov.-Dec. 10am-5pm;
Mar.-Dec. closed Tue.Jan.-
Feb. Fri.-Mon. 11am-5pm;
closed Easter, Thanksgiving,
Christmas, New Year's Day

Brush up on your wine knowledge along the Parkway.

BARBOURSVILLE VINEYARDS
17655 Winery Rd.
PO Box 136
Barboursville, VA 22923
(540) 832-3824
www.barboursvillewine.com
Open: Mon-Sat, 10am-
5pm; Sun, 11am-5pm

**CARDINAL POINT
VINEYARD AND WINERY**
9423 Batesville Rd.
Afton, VA 22920
(540) 456-8400
www.cardinalpointwinery.com
Open: Feb.-Dec. 11am-
5:30pm Daily; Jan. 11am-
5:30pm weekends/by appt.;
closed New Year's Day,
Easter, Thanksgiving and
Christmas

**DELFOSSE VINEYARDS
AND WINERY**
500 DelFosse Winery Ln.
Faber, VA 22938
(434) 263-6100
www.delfossewine.com
Opening May 2005; Call
for details.

FIRST COLONY WINERY
1650 Harris Creek Rd.,
Charlottesville, VA 22920
(877) 979-7105
www.firstcolonywinery.com
Open: Daily 11am-5pm

**HILL TOP BERRY FARM
AND WINERY**
2800 Berry Hill Rd.,
Nellysford, VA 22958
(434) 361-1266
www.hilltopberrywine.com
Open: Wed.-Sat. 11am-
5pm; Sun. 1pm-5pm

HORTON CELLARS WINERY
6399 Spotswood Trl.,
Gordonsville, VA 22942
(800) 829-4633
www.hvwine.com
Open: Daily 10am-5pm

JEFFERSON VINEYARDS
1353 Thomas Jefferson Pkwy.,
Charlottesville, VA 22902
(800) 272-3042
www.jeffersonvineyards.com
Open: Daily 11am-5pm

KING FAMILY VINEYARDS
6550 Roseland Farm

Crozet, VA 22932
(434) 823-7800
www.kingfamilyvineyards.com
Open: Daily 11am-5pm

**KLUGE ESTATE WINERY
AND VINEYARD**
100 Grand Cru Dr. and
3550 Blenheim Rd.
Charlottesville, VA 22902
(434) 977-3895
www.klugeestate.com
Open: Farm Shop/Tasting
Room Tue.-Sun. 10am-5pm

**OAKENCROFT VINEYARD &
WINERY**
1486 Oakencroft Ln.
Charlottesville, VA 22901
(434) 296-4188
www.oakencroft.com
Open: Apr.-Dec 11am-5pm
Daily; Mar. weekends only
11am-5pm

VERITAS WINERY
145 Saddleback Farm
Afton, VA 22920
(540) 456-8000
www.veritaswines.com
Open: Daily 11am-5pm

WHITE HALL VINEYARDS
5282 Sugar Ridge Rd.
White Hall, VA 22987
(434) 823-8615
www.whitehallvineyards.com
Open: Wed.-Sun. 11am-
5pm; Closed Dec. 15-Mar. 1

WINTERGREEN WINERY
PO Box 648; 462 Winery Ln.
Nellysford 22958
(434) 361-2519
www.WintergreenWinery.com
Open: Daily year-round;
Apr.-Oct. 10am-6pm; Nov.-
Mar. 10am-5pm

Plan a winery tour along the Blue Ridge Parkway.

1 H *Please refer to map*

PAT & CHUCK BLACKLEY

Enjoy the best of the mountains and the lake at Smith Mountain Lake, with activities ranging from fishing and boating, to hiking and hunting.

Smith Mountain Lake

16430 Booker T. Washington Hwy. #2
Moneta, VA 24121
(800) 676-8203
(540) 721-1203
www.visitsmithmountainlake.com
•MP 121.4, U.S. 220, U.S. 460

Smith Mountain Lake has over 22,000 acres of water with 500 miles of shoreline. Boating, fishing and other water recreation draw families on vacation, retirees and year-round residents to the lakeshore. Plenty of dining options, unique shops and accommodations ranging from full-service inns to rustic cabins draw visitors to the area for more than one stay.

continued from page 42

Normandy, honored at the National D-Day Memorial

History abounds in Bedford. The town is home to the **National D-Day Memorial**, remembering the 35 sons the town sent to Normandy – 21 were lost, the highest per capita loss from any area in the nation. (540) 587-3619.

Historic sites include: **Avenel**, an 1838 home on a 200-acre plantation; **Bedford Historic District, Bedford County Courthouse, Bedford City/County Museum** and **Bedford Meeting House**. See box on page 44 for more information.

Wineries

PAT & CHUCK BLACKLEY

Hill Top Berry Farm and Winery was originally opened as a pick-your-own blackberry farm; it was expanded into a winery in the late 1990s.

Thomas Jefferson first planted grapes for Virginia wine in his vineyards at Monticello, and many local vineyard owners are continuing the tradition. Charlottesville and the surrounding counties are rich in vineyards and wineries, which often combine Old World charm with modern agricultural techniques. In fact, the area is home to many medal-winning wines and our wineries provide visitors with opportunities for tastings, catered dinners, barbecues and winery tours. Virginia's fine wines are suitable for the most influential and discerning people such as Presidents Reagan and Clinton, who have served Oakencroft Vineyard wines at state dinners and summit conferences. Reagan even gave Oakencroft wine to Mikhail Gorbachev.

See page 46 for more winery information.

Virginia's Blue Ridge Highlands

Parkway MP 116 to 216.9 (VA–NC state line)
Galax • Pulaski • Abingdon • Floyd • Rocky Mount • Marion • Bristol

The magic of the undiscovered is supreme in this part of Virginia. The trails, mile-high peaks (with wild ponies) of Mount Rogers National Recreation Area soar above the birthplace of Country Music. In the little towns of the region, old-timey music rings out as it did deep into the last century.

Mountain Music is a staple as constant and true as the mountains in Virginia's Blue Ridge Highlands. Galax is home of the annual Old Fiddlers' Convention and a weekly live radio bluegrass show. The Blue Ridge Music Center, near Fishersville, brings the music to life with summer concerts. Floyd Country Store hosts live mountain music each week and County Records, in the old Floyd Picture theater, is the largest distributor of bluegrass and mountain music in the world. The Birthplace of Country Music is marked with a museum in Bristol. Also in these beautiful hills you'll find the State Theater of Virginia, fine dining, NASCAR racing and beautiful miles of the Blue Ridge Parkway.

Fiddlers and other musicians gather at Galax each August.

PAT & CHUCK BLACKLEY

◁   *Still a working gristmill, Mabry Mill, at MP 176.1 also offers events and dining right on the parkway.*

Grayson Highlands State Park's 5,000 acres
include restored structures in the Homestead area.

Getting Around

The Parkway is roughly paralleled, about 40 miles to the west, by I-81 and old U.S. 11, which are the major north-south routes through the region. I-77 cuts through the region from Bluefield, at the W.Va. line, to the N.C. line just south of Galax. U.S. 58 runs east-west across the lower reaches of the region and U.S. 460 performs a similar role across the north.

Key

▬	Blue Ridge Parkway
▬	Skyline Drive
▬	Highways
—	Secondary Roads
▬	Rivers/Lakes
▲	Overlooks
⁝⁝	Tunnels
MP	Mileposts ⑰
🥤	Gasoline
👫	Restrooms
🍴	Food
⌇	Picnicking
⛪	Visitor Center
🌲	State Park

•West of Blacksburg, you will find Mountain Lake, one of Virginia's only two natural lakes, at 4,000 feet above sea level. The area is also home to UVA's Mountain Lake Biological Station.

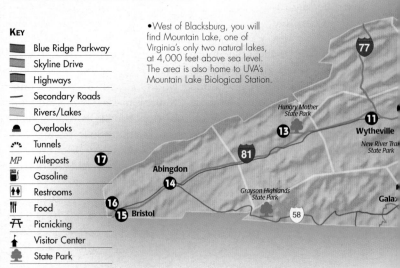

Hungry Mother State Park

Wytheville

New River Trail State Park

⑪

⑬

81

Abingdon

⑭

Grayson Highlands State Park

58

Gala⟩

⑯

⑮ Bristol

•The westernmost tip of Southwest Virginia is further west than Detroit.

•Eleanor Roosevelt spent her summers in Abingdon as a girl and later helped Abingdon's Barter Theatre become the State Theatre of Virginia.

•Burkes Garden, in Tazewell County and nicknamed "God's Thumbprint" for its bowl-like geography, was the first choice of George Vanderbilt for the home that would become Biltmore Estate in Asheville. Locals refused to sell him land.

These small cabins at Rocky Knob are available for travelers.

Bluegrass Music Lives Here

The Old Fiddlers' Convention in Galax is the largest event of its kind in the world and attracts 50,000 people annually. Many come from as far away as Europe and Japan. Not surprising, perhaps is that Southwestern Virginia is the birthplace of bluegrass and country music and is home of many music legends such as Ralph Stanley and the Carter Family. The new Blue Ridge Music Center near MP 213 and Galax will further celebrate the tradition.

•Virginia's highest peak – Mt. Rogers – looms atop this region at 5,729 feet.

•The New River is among the oldest rivers in the world. Part of the evidence: It flows south to north.

DOUG MILLER

The restaurant at Château Morrisette offers fine food and a wide range of wine styles (MP171.5).

•New River Trail State Park offers a 57-mile rail-trail between Pulaski and Galax. (Bike rentals available.)

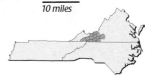

10 miles

•Franklin County, centered on Rocky Mount, bears the dubious distinction of being labeled by the ATF "rev'noors" as the Moonshine Capital of the United States.

SIGHTS AND SITES AT A GLANCE

❶ Blue Ridge Institute & Museum
❷ Blacksburg/ Christiansburg
❸ Mountain Lake Resort
❹ Floyd County
❺ Chateau Morrisette Winery
❻ Mabry Mill (also see p. 5)
❼ Mayberry Trading Post

❽ Doe Run Lodge/Resort
❾ Hillsville
❿ Fort Chiswell Outlets
⓫ Wytheville
⓬ Galax
  ⓬ᴀ Blue Ridge Music Center
  ⓬ʙ New River Trail State Park
  ⓬ᴄ Rex Theatre

⓭ Hungry Mother State Park
⓮ Barter Theatre
⓯ Birthplace of Country Music Museum
⓰ Carter Family Fold
⓱ Ralph Stanley Museum

See also:
  Traveler Services p. 59
  Trip Planner Listing p.130

🍀 For specific locations of state parks see www.dcr.state.va.us/parks or call (800) 933-PARK.

Blue Ridge Institute & Museum ❶

Ferrum College, PO Box 1000,
Va. 40W, Ferrum, VA 24088
(540) 365-4416
bri@ferrum.edu
www.blueridgeinstitute.org
•MP 121.5, take U.S. 220 to
Va. 40
•Designated the state center for
Blue Ridge Folklore by VA
General Assembly

The Highlands area is home to many small town agricultural fairs showcasing local livestock and regional foods.

Located at Ferrum College, the museum documents, interprets and presents the traditional life and culture of the Blue Ridge. BRI includes a working German-American farm museum from 1800, Blue Ridge Heritage Archives – a repository for the preservation of materials related to area folklife plus gallery exhibits. The annual Blue Ridge Folklife Festival, the state's largest celebration of folklife, is held in October.

Blacksburg/ Christiansburg ❷

Montgomery County Chamber
of Commerce
612 New River Road
New River Valley Mall
Christiansburg, VA 24073
(540) 382-4010
www.montgomerycc.org
•MP 165, take Va. 8 to
U.S. 460

The historic town of Blacksburg dates from 1797 when an area resident donated 38 acres of land to form a village. Blacksburg incorporated into a town a year later. In the mid-1800s, a small Methodist school was established that later became Virginia Polytechnic Institute and State University, commonly known as Virginia Tech. From its humble beginnings as a land grant college in 1872, the university has grown into a major research

facility, with more than 25,000 students and a nationally ranked football team. The campus is of particular architectural interest, as most of the buildings are faced in what is known as "hokie stone" after the school's mascot. Neo-Gothic architecture in locally quarried stone surrounding a large open grassy area, or the "drillfield," in the center of the campus makes for one of the prettiest university locations in the state.

Great restaurants, shopping and sightseeing can be found in the Blacksburg area, 30 miles off the Park-

Mountain Lake Hotel's Sunday brunch has become a favorite tradition for many.

way from Floyd. It is also the halfway point between the Parkway and Mountain Lake Hotel.

Mountain Lake Hotel ❸

115 Hotel Circle
Pembroke, VA 24136
(800) 346-3334
(540) 626-7121
info@mountainlakehotel.com
www.mountainlakehotel.com
•MP 165, take Va. 8 to U.S.
460 to Va. 700
•Featured in the film "Dirty
Dancing"

For over 150 years, this 2,600-acre mountaintop resort has welcomed guests. "Do it all or do nothing at all" is the hotel's promise to its guests who can hike, fish, swim, enjoy hayrides or carriage jaunts at the resort. Or, those so inclined can just enjoy the view. The resort boasts 20 types of accommodations from cottages to the lodge. For more information see box on this page.

Floyd County ❹

210 B S. Locust St., PO Box 510
Floyd, Va. 24091
(540) 745-4407
chamber@swva.net
www.visitfloyd.org
•MP 165.35, Va. 8

Begin your tour of Floyd County at the only stoplight – it's a great starting point in this county of musicians, artists and craftspeople. The largest distributor of bluegrass and mountain music in the world, **County Records**, is located in the former Floyd Picture Theater. **The Old Church Gallery** exhibits works of local artists; **June Bug Center** is a craft co-op.

Chateau Morrisette wines get some of their flavor from oak barrels that come from both French and American forests

COURTESY CHATEAU MORRISETTE

Chateau Morrisette Winery ❺

PO Box 766
Meadows of Dan,
VA 24120
(540) 593-2865
Fax: (540) 593-2868
info@chateaumorrisette.com
www.thedogs.com
•MP 171.5

With 20 years of winemaking, **Chateau Morrisette Winery** in Floyd County has garnered many awards such as the Virginia

Mountain Lake Hotel

Have the Time of Your Life

Take some time to enjoy the little things in life; a little time with family, a little time to yourselves, a little bit of the great outdoors and a whole lot of memories. Experience a piece of heaven, some say, for peace of mind. "Dirty Dancing" was filmed here! 2,600 acre family resort with hiking, boating, fishing, tennis, swimming, lawn games, entertainment, children's programs and so much more! For a great family vacation or a romantic getaway, you can have the time of your life at Mountain Lake.

Come to Mountain Lake to indulge your senses.

utes from Parkway
Open: Reg. Season: May-Oct., Thanksgiving; weekends in Nov. Winter Season: year-round in our new Blueberry Ridge Cottages only
Rates: Specials/packages
For more info:
Mountain Lake Hotel
115 Hotel Cir.
Pembroke, VA 24136
(800) 828-0490
(540) 626-7121
www.mountainlakehotel.com

Traveler info:
Distance: Approx. 50 min-
❸ *Please refer to map*

Discover Carroll County's Treasures and Historic Hillsville

Visit for a Day. Stay for a Lifetime.

With its incredible natural beauty, friendly people, interesting sites to explore, and host of year-round activities to enjoy, we are a great place to visit. We offer 30 miles of spectacular scenery along the parkway with such features as the Ground Hog Mountain Overlook, Orlean Puckett Cabin, Fancy Gap and the Blue Ridge Music Center. Nearby are Historic Downtown Hillsville, Southwest Virginia Regional Farmers' Market, arts and crafts, and New River Trail State Park. Request our brochure.

Buffalo Mountain can be viewed through much of the county. Photo by Chris Martin.

Traveler info:
Distance: Between MP 182 and 212
For more info:
Carroll County Office of Tourism
605-1 Pine St.
Hillsville, VA 24343
I-77 Exits 8 and 14
(888) 785-2781
CarrollTourism@ChillsNet.org
www.ChillsNet.org

❾ *Please refer to map*

Experience the best in outlet shopping when you spend a day at The Village.

Ft. Chiswell Outlets

Spend A Day At The Village

Nestled in the beautiful Blue Ridge Mountains, the view surrounding our village of shops is almost as impressive as the great savings! Conveniently located at the crossroads of interstates I-77 and I-81, the Ft. Chiswell Outlets offer a large selection of top-quality brands at up to 70% off regular department store prices! Reebok, Polo Ralph Lauren, Hush Puppies and Van Heusen are just a few of the great reasons to Spend a Day at the Village!

Traveler info:
Distance: 25 miles from Parkway
Open: Jan.-Feb. Mon.-Thur. 10am-6pm, Fri.-Sat. 10am-8pm, Sun. Noon-6pm; Mar.-Dec. Mon.-Sat. 9am-8pm, Sun. Noon-6pm
For more info:
Ft. Chiswell Outlets
731 Factory Outlet Drive
Max Meadows, VA 24360
(276) 637-6214
www.ftchiswelloutlets.com

10 *Please refer to map*

KEN DUNN

Mount Rogers, in Grayson County, is Virginia's highest peak, at 5,729 feet.

State Fair Best in Show and the Governor's Cup Award-Winning Wines. Enjoy a wine-tasting tour here and stop by the restaurant for lunch or dinner featuring fresh baked bread, desserts and, of course, wine.

Mabry Mill **6**

266 Mabry Mill Rd. SE
Meadows of Dan, VA 24120
(276) 952-2947
www.nps.gov/blri/rockknob.htm
•MP 176.1

Mabry Mill, one of the most photographed sites on the parkway, is a restored gristmill and sawmill from the early part of this century. Old time skills such as weaving are presented at the site and old time bluegrass music is played on Sundays. A coffee shop and cabins are nearby. See box on page 5 for more info.

Mayberry Trading Post **7**

883 Mayberry Church Rd.
Meadows of Dan, VA 24120
(276) 952-2155
www.co.patrick.va.us
•MP 180-181

Mayberry Trading Post, built in 1892, was originally home to the post office and a general store. Still a country store with original counter boards from the late 1800s, the trading post features homemade molasses, apple butter, mountain crafts, toys and books about the area. Open all year-the proprietors say browsers are welcome.

Doe Run Lodge **8**

PO Box 280
Fancy Gap, VA 24328
(800) 325-6189
(276) 398-2212
info@doerunlodge.com
www.doerunlodge.com
•MP 189

Located on Groundhog Mountain at MP 189 between Meadows of Dan and Fancy Gap, Doe Run Lodge is one of the few places of lodging located directly on the Blue Ridge Parkway. An alpine lodge, cliffside chalets and poolside villas make for varied lodging with a great view. Amenities include a restaurant, swimming, golf and tennis.

The Blue Ridge Music Center at Fishers Peak (MP 213) hosts concerts all summer.

Galax ⑫

Galax-Carroll-Grayson
Chamber of Commerce
608 West Stuart Dr.
Galax, VA 24333
(276) 236-2184
email@gcgchamber.com
www.gcgchamber.com
•MP 215.8, take VA 89

Outdoor recreation at three state parks surrounds the town of Galax. Delve into history at Jeff Matthews Memorial Museum, a log cabin filled with artifacts.

Bluegrass music is important to Galax. The **Old Fiddlers' Convention**, said to be the world's largest and oldest, is held annually in August. "Blue Ridge Backroads," one of only three live "old-time" bluegrass radio shows, is broadcast every Friday evening from the **Rex Theater**.

Blue Ridge Music Center ⑫ A

Fishers Peak, MP 213
608 West Stuart Dr.
Galax, VA 24333
(276) 236-5309
drobinson@galaxcity.org
www.nps.gov/blri/BRMC.htm
www.blueridgemusiccenter.net
•MP 213, 12 miles from Galax

The city of Galax gave 1,000 acres to the Blue Ridge Parkway to provide a home for the Blue Ridge Music Center for the preservation and interpretation of regional music. Located at the base of Fishers Peak, the facility plans included an amphitheater and instrument builders' workshop. Concerts are held each summer.

Mountain Music

Fiddling is a fine tradition in the Appalachians, with technique passed down through the generations.

Old-time music is as much for participating in as for watching. Festivals, teaching workshops and informal get-togethers keep this music alive.

Played on acoustic instruments, the mountain-type folk music of the Southern Appalachians includes old English ballads, old fiddle tunes, and Civil War-era banjo tunes.

Fiddles were small enough instruments for immigrants from the British Isles to bring with them. The ballads, folk-songs and dance tunes they played have been passed down through generations. Then the banjo of the minstrel shows was introduced during the time of the Civil War and changed the sound and style.

This early country music spread as the Grand Ole Opry and radio made stars out of local musicians such as the Carter Family.

After the Depression, guitars replaced fiddles and banjos and the music grew into what is now popular country music.

Old-time music still has a following, though, for people who like the traditional sounds and appreciate its continuity with the past.

Wytheville, Virginia

Small Town, Big Experience

Historic Wytheville

Spend a few hours or a few days and discover the interesting attractions and friendly spirit that has put this town on the map. All ages will enjoy the natural, historic, and man-made attractions. From an animal park to an Indian village, from musical theatre to Civil War attractions, from antiques to a pioneer town, the Wytheville area is full of things to see and do. Located at the intersection of interstates 77 & 81, it's sure to fit into your Parkway experience.

Traveler info:
Distance: 35 miles from Parkway
For more info:
Wytheville Convention & Visitors Bureau
975 Tazewell St.
Wytheville, VA 24382
(877) 347-8307
www.VisitWytheville.com

⑪ *Please refer to map*

The Crooked Road ~ Virginia's Heritage Music Trail

It's A Feast for the ears. A feast for the eyes. A feast for one's very soul.

Wind through glorious mountains, where music floats over the ridge and settles upon you like the soundtrack to your very own adventure. Send for your guide and follow this new trail. Follow The Crooked Road – Virginia's Heritage Music Trail.

They say if you follow any American music to its source – blues, jazz or country, one of its deepest roots is likely to reach a spot near this place. There is so much to take in – sweet mountain music, friendly people, arts & crafts, food, hiking, and jaw-dropping scenery.

Highlights include the Blue Ridge Institute & Museum at Ferrum, which presents the culture of the Blue Ridge and its people and houses one of the nation's premier collections of heritage music. Each fall the campus of Ferrum College hosts a "Top 20 Event in the Southeast"

The Carter Family Fold provides terrific family entertainment.

Daniel Womack: The Blue Ridge Music Institute showcases a variety of musicians throughout the year.

with the Blue Ridge Folklife festival. A stop at the Floyd Country Store on a Friday night is guaranteed fun when everyone is invited to dance to live music. But any day of the week is a fine time to explore this charming small town.

Follow the trail through miles of mountain beauty to the Rex Theater in Galax or the Blue Ridge Music Center nearby for live performances. From Ricky Skaggs to local favorites the music is toe-tappin and the crowds are friendly. Each August Galax plays host to the world's oldest and largest fiddler's convention. This unique week-long celebration has attracted thousands of music lovers and hundreds of musicians for seventy years.

And no visit to The Crooked Road would be complete without a visit to Bristol – known as the birthplace of country music.

A must-see spot is the famous Carter Family Fold in rural Hiltons. The Carter family, who are considered by many to be country music's first family, provide family oriented shows with all acoustic music and plenty of dancing.

The Blue Ridge Music Center offers a wonderful setting for music on summer weekends.

1 12 A 12 C *Please refer to map*

The Crooked Road ~ Virginia's Heritage Music Trail

A National Historic Landmark located near Norton, the Country Cabin is a great place to hear music. Local and regional musicians gather each Saturday night to perform country and bluegrass music.

New to the trail is the Ralph Stanley Museum in Clintwood, which honors the Grammy-winning star of the "Oh Brother Where Art Thou" CD. His annual festival each Memorial Day weekend draws fans from around the world.

Send for your free guide to Virginia's Heritage Music Trail complete with a map and a variety of lodging choices along with details about many other attractions and an annual music festivals calendar. From the Ralph Stanley Festival to the Old Time Fiddlers Convention; from the Dock Boggs Festival to the live radio broadcasts at the Rex Theater – Send for your copy of this NEW guide and start planning your trip on the Crooked Road.

Call 866-MTN-MUSIC

The Birthplace of Country Music Alliance Museum in Bristol provides a unique way to view musical artifacts and learn about the history of country music.

Send for your free visitors guide with event calendar and map. For additional information, call 866-MTN-MUSIC.

(866-686-6874) to receive your Free Guide.

Traveler info:
Distance: From zero to 150 miles from Parkway
Open: Daily
Rates: Varies by location &

For more info:
Heart of Appalachia
The Crooked Road
P.O. Box 268
Big Stone Gap, VA 24219
(866) MTN-MUSIC
www.thecrookedroad.org
info@thecrookedroad.org

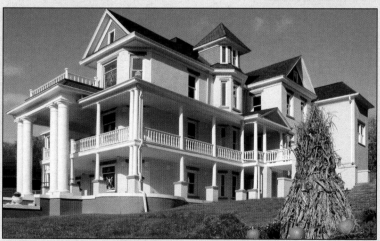

The state-of-the-art interactive Ralph Stanley Museum is housed in this beautiful Clintwood home.

   Please refer to map

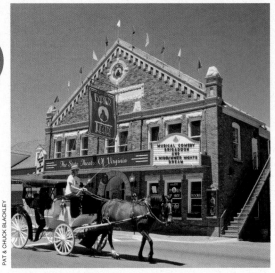

PAT & CHUCK BLACKLEY

Barter Theater got its name because farmers would barter produce in exchange for tickets to productions.

Park in Smyth County is named for an Indian legend. Swimming and paddleboating are popular on the park lake. Other features include a full-service restaurant, conference center, cabins, camping and interpretive programs such as canoe tours and nature hikes.

Barter Theatre ⓮

133 W. Main St., P.O. Box 867
Abingdon, VA 24212
Box office: (276) 628-3991
barterinfo@bartertheatre.com
www.bartertheatre.com
•MP 177.7, take U.S. 58
•Oldest Repertory Theater in America

Many careers were launched at Barter Theatre including those of Gregory Peck, Patricia Neal, Ernest Borgnine. Many visitors have been introduced to professional theater at Barter, first opened by Robert Porterfield in 1933. Named the State Theatre of Virginia in 1946, Barter is home to the

New River Trail State Park ⓬ B

176 Orphanage Dr.
Foster Falls, VA 24360
(276) 699-6778
Reservations: (800) 933-PARK or reserve online
www.dcr.state.va.us/parks/newriver.htm
•Several entrances: by Galax MP 215.8, then VA 89 to US 58 (parking is available where 58 crosses Chestnut Creek)
•Parallels 39 miles of the New River

This 57-mile long state park is part of the Rails to Trails program and follows an abandoned railroad right-of-way. There are several entrances to the park as it meanders through four Virginia counties. The trail uses two tunnels, three major bridges and 30 minor bridges and trestles. A historic shot tower, where ammunition was made, is nearby.

Hungry Mother State Park ⓭

2854 Park Blvd.
Marion, Va. 24354-9323,
(276) 781-7400
Reservations: (800) 933-PARK or reserve online

www.dcr.state.va.us/parks/hungrymo.htm
•MP 199.1, take US 52 to I-77 to I-81 Exit 47 to VA 16

One of 6 original CCC camps opened in 1936, Hungry Mother State

SU CLAUSON-WICKER

The New River Trail crosses the Hiwassee bridge two miles from Allisonia.

COURTESY NETTA

Bristol Tenn./Va., the birthplace of country music, was the site of the first recording studio built specifically to record old-time mountain, or country music.

summer time Appalachian Festival of Plays and Playwrights.

Birthplace of Country Music Museum ⑮

Bristol Mall/500 Gate City Hwy.
Bristol, VA 24201
(276) 645-0035
www.birthplaceofcountrymusic.org
•MP 291.9, take U.S. 321 to U.S. 421
•Dave Loggins, of "Please Come to Boston" fame is also from Bristol

The year was 1927, and music was fast becoming a popular commodity. Record playing machines – some electric and some hand-cranked – were making music heard in even the remotest households all across America. In places like the mountains of Virginia, old-time country musicians like the Fiddlin' Powers family from Scott County and Ernest Stoneman of Galax were making

their reputations known. Still, most had to go to places like New York and New Jersey to find recording studios in which to make the records. Record producer Ralph Peer, however, had a better idea – bring the studio to the mountains.

Peer placed ads in the newspaper seeking local talent. Success came quickly. As one newspaper would later report, "In no other section of the South have the pre-war melodies and old mountaineer songs been better preserved than in the mountains of East Tennessee and Southwest Virginia."

The Carter Family, Jimmy Rogers, Carter and Ralph Stanley and so many others got their start in Bristol.

In October of 1998, the Congress of the United States recognized Bristol as "The Birthplace of Country Music" and work was soon begun on a fitting site for its memorial.

BLUE RIDGE HIGHLANDS SERVICES

CHATEAU MORRISETTE

MP 171.5 • PO Box 766 • Meadows of Dan, VA 24120 • (540) 593-2865 • E-Mail: info@thedogs.com • Open Daily

Chateau Morrisette brings unique style and character to premium wines and fine dining. Daily tours of winery and tasting room. Enjoy lunch and dinner in our restaurant (reservations requested). Make plans to visit us today.

www.thedogs.com

www.visitgalax.com

THE CITY OF GALAX

Distance: Approx. 10 miles from Parkway • 111 E. Grayson St. • Galax, VA • (276) 238-8130

Come share the tradition of Old-time and Bluegrass music in the Heart of the Blue Ridge. Extend your Parkway visit into Galax and share our music, mountain culture, crafts, and shopping. Rent bicycles or horses to explore the beauty of the New River Trail State Park. We're preserving our history through music, nature, and hospitality.

HOLIDAY INN HOTEL AND SUITES BRISTOL CONVENTION CENTER

Distance: 65 miles from Parkway • 3005 Linden Dr.. • Bristol, VA 24202 • (888) 466-4141 • E-mail: dkeithan@trammellproperties.com • AE, DC, MC, V, Diners Club • ♿

An award winning full-service hotel featuring 224 deluxe rooms and suites, plus an outdoor pool, whirlpool and a fitness center.

RAMADA INN WYTHEVILLE

Distance: 40 miles from Parkway • 955 Peppers Ferry Rd. • Wytheville, VA 24382 • (276) 228-6000 • 154 rooms • AE, V, MC, D • ♿

Ramada offers in-room cable TV, coffee makers, hairdryers, irons and ironing boards. Country Kitchen restaurant and the Victory Lane Lounge are located here on property. Visitors will find the best in golf, recreation, antiques, shopping and local attractions.

www.ramadawytheville.com

www.smythchamber.org

SMYTH COUNTY, HUNGRY MOTHER, GRAYSON HIGHLANDS

Distance: Approx. 50 miles from Parkway • 214 West Main St. • Marion, VA 24354 • (276) 783-3161 • E-mail: smythcofc@netva.com

Rich in Civil War history, home of Mount Rogers NRA and Hungry Mother State Park, which offers campsites, cabins, boating and beach. Appalachian Trail access including Grayson Highlands State Park, which offers camping and horse/hiking trails.

TOWN OF ROCKY MOUNT

Distance: Approx. 20 miles from Parkway • 345 Donald Ave. • Rocky Mount, VA 24151 • (540) 483-0907 • E-mail: lburleson@rockymountva.org

Small town charm is highlighted with our lavish farmers market, offering the freshest produce, and a visit to our welcoming hospitality center. Bordered by serene farmlands and majestic forested ridges, Rocky Mount is a thriving small town. Rocky Mount, Virginia, a little uptown...a little downtown...a lot to offer!

www.rockymountva.org

Pinnacle Living Magazine

Life Is Good In The Mountains

Cool, clean, safe and uncrowded. Pinnacle Living Magazine invites you to step inside our mountain dream homes with a FREE copy of our current issue.

Let us sweep you into a world filled with calm relaxation, renewed spirit and page after page of inspiring hilltop hideaways.

As beautiful as it is informative, you'll get great advice – from where to find the hottest new mountain communities to tips on how to create mountain style from couples who've already found that perfect retreat. That perfect family gathering place.

Find new ways to celebrate the seasons and the milestones with design and decorating ideas that speak of healthy mountain vitality. Meet artisans. Shop antiques. Bring the spirit of the mountains into your life, no matter where you live.

Gain private entry into magnificent mountain

Get a private glance inside fabulous southern mountain homes for decorating and design ideas.

manors. Take a peek at these gorgeous homes and you'll find scores of appeal-

Call for your FREE issue today! 1-800-548-1672, ext. 4044.

ing ideas. From a country barn cleverly remodeled as a spectacular second home, to a majestic timber hilltop cabin, to a lakeside contemporary designed with a view from every room.

Not only will you discover the best areas to find a second home in the mountains of North Carolina, Virginia, Tennessee, South Carolina, Georgia, West Virginia and Maryland, but you'll also get great advice on real estate investments, whether buying or building.

With detailed charts of 100+ communities in these southern states, Pinnacle Living provides you the resources you need to find that perfect mountain retreat.

Call for your FREE current copy of Pinnacle Living and find your Southern-mountain dream-home. 1-800-548-1672, ext. 4044.

Find planning, building and decorating advice from couples who have already found their dream home.

For more info:
Pinnacle Living
3424 Brambleton Ave. SW
Roanoke, VA 24018
(800) 548-1672, Ext. 4044
circ@leisurepublishing.com
www.pinnacleliving.net

North Carolina's High Country

Parkway MP 216.9 to 337
Mount Airy • Wilkesboro • Boone • Valle Crucis • Banner Elk • Beech Mountain • Blowing Rock • Linville • Little Switzerland

There's a great contrast in scale in this part of the mountains. Quaint villages such as Little Switzerland and Blowing Rock dot the countryside beneath the majesty of the peaks that give the region its nickname – the High Country.

The village of Blowing Rock's artistic bent, the old-fashioned charm of Mast General Store, the excitement of the mile-high swinging bridge on Grandfather Mountain – all are hints of the limitless fun and natural bounty of the High Country. Nature is preserved here, crafts are taught to new generations and mountain music rings out on summer nights. Recreation can range from snow skiing on Beech Mountain to driving up the Linn Cove Viaduct as it heads for the sky at Grandfather Mountain. The town that inspired "The Andy Griffith Show" is here, as are the amazing frescoes of Ashe County and the stunning natural beauty of the Linville Falls area. The last piece of the Blue Ridge Parkway to be completed – the graceful Linn Cove Viaduct – is also here, as part of the high-country miles of the parkway through this region.

JOHNNY MEEKS

Main Street, Blowing Rock: The restaurants have earned it the nickname "The Calabash of the Mountains."

◁ *The Linn Cove Viaduct, completed in 1987, was the last section of the parkway to be constructed; MP 304.*

Getting Around

The Blue Ridge Parkway bisects the High Country. Try the Parkway for a guaranteed scenic drive with stops such as MP 304.4 at Linn Cove Viaduct, MP 291.9 at Blowing Rock and MP 258.7 at Glendale Springs. As you pass the weathered barns of highland farms, you'll feel the High Country's special quiet.

State-designated Scenic Byways in the region include New River Valley Byway (N.C. 194 from Boone to Baldwin and N.C. 16/88 east of Jefferson to Laurel Springs); Mission Crossing (N.C. 194 from Elk Park to Valle Crucis to Vilas); and Little Parkway (U.S. 221 between Blowing Rock and Linville also called Yonalossee Trail).

J. SCOTT BRAHAM

The Blowing Rock is the site of winds that carry things upward.

KEY

■	Blue Ridge Parkway
■	Skyline Drive
■	Highways
—	Secondary Roads
■	Rivers/Lakes
▲	Overlooks
⁂	Tunnels
MP	Mileposts
■	Gasoline
♦♦	Restrooms
⅄	Food
开	Picnicking
♠	Visitor Center
♣	State Park

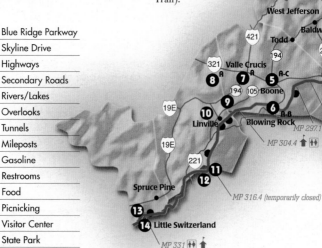

West Jefferson
Baldwin
Todd
Valle Crucis
Boone
Linville
Blowing Rock
Spruce Pine
Little Switzerland

MP 294.1
MP 297.1
MP 304.4
MP 316.4 (temporarily closed)
MP 331

VICKI ROZEMA

• In 1872, a Mt. Airy farmer sold a rocky section in his newly purchased acreage; the "worthless" parcel ended up becoming the world's largest open-faced granite mine.

• In Zionville, near the Tennessee state line, the Old Buffalo Trail, over which herds of buffalo once migrated, intersects Daniel Boone's Trail, over which settlers heading west migrated.

Mast Farm General Store in Valle Crucis was established in 1883; its interior appears much as it did then.

Linn Cove Viaduct: The Last Parkway Piece

The Linn Cove Viaduct, completed in 1987 (MP 304.4) and one of the most complicated concrete bridges ever built, was the last piece of the Blue Ridge Parkway built, more than 20 years after all but those 7.5 miles. It is one of the most photographed spots in the eastern U.S. The bridge, curling around Grandfather Mountain, includes a dozen parking overlooks and the 13.5-mile Tanawha Trail. The beautiful views and thrilling drive toward the sky around Grandfather make the Linn Cove Viaduct an attraction in itself.

•The Black Mountains, a 15-mile-long horseshoe of peaks from Boone to Mt. Mitchell, contain some of the highest peaks in the Blue Ridge. They were named "black" by early settlers because of the dark fir trees covering their slopes.

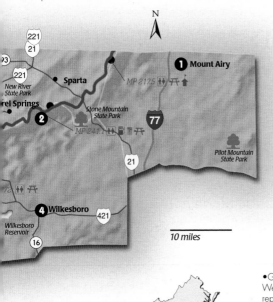

The Cone Mansion is the centerpiece of Moses H. Cone Memorial Park at MP 293-295.5.

VICKIE ROZEMA

•Grandfather Mountain's U.S. Weather Service Station has been reporting conditions daily since 1955. The highest wind speed recorded at its summit was 195 mph on April 18, 1995.

SIGHTS AND SITES AT A GLANCE

① Mount Airy
② Doughton Park/ Bluffs Lodge (p. 5)
③ Frescoes
④ Eddy Merle Watson Garden & MerleFest
⑤ Boone
  ⑤ A Appalachian Cultural Museum
  ⑤ B Holiday Inn Express

⑤ C "Horn in the West"
⑥ Blowing Rock
  ⑥ A Parkway Craft Center/Flat Top Manor at Cone Park
  ⑥ B Tweetsie Railroad
⑦ Valle Crucis
  A Mast General Store
⑧ Beech Mountain
  ⑨ A Inns of Beech Mountain

⑨ DeWoolfson Down
⑩ Grandfather Mountain
⑪ Linville Gorge Wilderness
⑫ Linville Caverns
⑬ Altapass Orchard
⑭ Switzerland Inn

See also:
Traveler Services p. 74
Trip Planner Listings p. 130

🌳 For specific locations of state parks see www.ils.unc.edu/parkproject/ncparks.html or call (919) 733-4181.

Mt. Airy   ❶

615 N. Main St.
Mt. Airy, NC 27030
(800) 576-0231
www.mtairyncchamber.org
www.visitmayberry.com
•MP 199.4, take U.S. 52 east
•More than 90 percent of visitors are following the Andy Griffith connection

Mt. Airy is more famous by another name: Mayberry. The television home of Andy, Opie and Aunt Bee was modeled after Mt. Airy. Actor Andy Griffith was born here and every September "Mayberry Days" is celebrated with special events. Stops in town include Floyd's Barber Shop and the Bluebird Diner, not to mention Pilot Mountain outside town (known as Mt. Pilot on the TV show).

The Frescoes of Glendale Springs ❸

PO Box 177
Glendale Springs, NC 28629
(336) 982-3076
(888) 343-2743
www.ashechamber.com
•MP 259
•Local families fed the artists, then became models for the frescoes

Doc Watson's musical heritage, and that of his son Merle, is kept alive each year at MerleFest in Wilkesboro.

Thousands of visitors make a pilgrimage each year to **Ashe County** to view the frescoes of Ben Long in the **Churches of the Frescoes** at **Glendale Springs**. **St. Mary's Church** has three frescoes: "Mary Great with Child," "John the Baptist" and "The Mystery of Faith" while **Holy Trinity Church** has "The Last Supper."

Eddy Merle Watson Garden & Merlefest   ❹

Wilkes Community College
1328 Collegiate Dr.
Wilkesboro, NC 28697

(336) 838-6100
www.merlefest.org
•From MP 276.4, take Hwy. 421 to Wilkesboro
•MerleFest features musicians from many genres

Eddy Merle Watson Garden of the Senses, on the campus of Wilkes Community College, is a memorial to the acoustic musician/son of Doc Watson, a blind musician. Designed so that everyone regardless of visual ability can enjoy it, the garden is funded by **MerleFest**. The annual acoustic music festival is held at the college and features an eclectic mix of over 100 artists (800) 343-7857.

"Horn in the West"   ❺c

PO Box 295
Boone, NC 28607
(828) 264-2120
www.horninthewest.com
•MP 291.9 Boone exit, US 221/321
•Tour Hickory Ridge Homestead as part of admission

For more than 50 summers, Kermit Hunter's drama of the American Revolution, **Horn in the West**, has come alive in **Boone**. Presented on three stages, the drama tells the story of late 18th-century mountain settlers and their role in the American Revolution. The adventures of Daniel Boone and his Mountain Men come alive in the drama. Mid-June-Mid-August.

Ben Long's frescoes, in two Episcopal churches in Ashe County, have been drawing visitors since the '70s.

Appalachian Cultural Museum/ Boone, N.C.  **5** ᴀ

Appalachian State University,
University Hall
Boone, NC 28608
(828) 262-3117
pinsoncg@appstate.edu
www.museum.appstate.edu
•Take the Boone exit from MP
291.9, then U.S. 221/321
Boone Convention & Visitors
Bureau
208 Howard Street
Boone, North Carolina 28607
(800) 852-9506
(828) 262-3516
info@VisitBooneNC.com
www.visitboonenc.com
•MP 276.4, take US 421 west

COURTESY SOUTHERN HIGHLAND CRAFT GUILD

The Parkway Craft Center Center displays the work of local artisans.

Appalachian Cultural Museum at Appalachian State University in Boone strives "to foster an understanding of the people and places of the Appalachian mountains" through exhibits of area history, geology, crafts and culture. Also included: Native American artifacts;

life in a mountain cabin; construction of the Blue Ridge Parkway and much more.

The Town of Boone, a magnet for snow skiers, has all the amenities of a small college town: unique dining, interesting shops, concerts and art galleries. See page 69 for more information.

Parkway Craft Center, Flat Top Manor at Cone Park  **6** ᴀ

667 Service Rd.
Blowing Rock, NC 28605
(828) 295-7938
parkwaycraft@skybest.com
www.southernhighlandguild.org

Boone and Beech Mountain Hotels

A Place For All Seasons

Holiday Inn Express – Winner of the 2004 Quality Excellence Award and the 2003 Development Award. 129 luxurious rooms including: double queen/ king rooms with Jacuzzi, and two room suites with fireplaces. A complimentary breakfast bar, outdoor heated pool, exercise room, 2-line phones with dataport, voice mail and high speed

Enjoy personal touches of home and our Southern hospitality.

wireless internet service. We can accommodate 10 to 100 people in our superb meeting facilities. Minutes from Grandfather Mountain, Tweetsie Railroad and all area attractions.

Traveler info:
Distance: Approx. 6 miles from Parkway
For more info:
Holiday Inn Express
1943 Blowing Rock
Boone, NC 28607
(888) 733-6867
(828) 264-2451
www.holidayinn-boone.com

The Inns of Beech Mountain – Beech Alpen Inn and Top of the Beech are two charming inns on top of scenic Beech Mountain. Offering rustic exposed beams, window seats, and fireplaces.

Experience perfection at its peak.

Complimentary continental breakfast. Area activities include hiking, whitewater rafting, golf, shopping, fly-fishing and snow skiing.

Traveler info:
Distance: Approx. 10 miles from Parkway
For more info:
The Beech Alpen Inn & Top of the Beech
700 Beech Mountain Pkwy.
Beech Mountain, NC 28604
(866) 284-2770
(828) 387-2252
www.beechalpen.com

5 ʙ **8** ᴀ *Please refer to map*

Caroline Brinegar's Cabin

MATTHEW & LORRIE JONES

The Brinegar Cabin is in Doughton Park, MP 241.1.

Caroline Brinegar was one of a "few old timers, sentimentally attached to their log cabins" who was granted a life-tenure lease on her home within the parkway boundary. The two-room cabin was built by Martin Brinegar in 1886, who considered the angle of the southern sun and the level of the building in creating an energy-efficient home. Caroline used a four-poster loom to weave linen and wool cloth for the family's clothes. The family, which included three children, also had an orchard, cornfield, vegetable garden, flax field, and a bee gum for honey.

A widow for the last 18 years of her life, she eventually moved down the mountain and spent the rest of her life living with relatives.

/parkwaycraft.html
www.nps.gov/blri/conepric.htm
•MP 294

History, crafts and recreation are blended at MP 294. **Moses H. Cone Memorial Park** has horseback riding, hiking trails and two lakes. The turn of the century **Flat Top Manor**, home of Moses and Bertha Cone, is a visitor center and home to a craft shop operated by Southern Highland Guild for a half-century. The work of local artists is on display and available for purchase. The combined parkland of Cone Park and adjacent **Julian Price Memorial Park** is the largest developed area along the Parkway.

Village of Blowing Rock ❻

Chamber of Commerce
PO Box 406
Blowing Rock, NC 28605
(800) 295-7851
(828) 295-7851
info@blowingrock.com

Wild West Family Fun At Tweetsie Railroad

Take a Trip Back to the Old West

As the Carolinas' original family theme park, Tweetsie Railroad is a unique attraction that allows children and families to explore their imaginations – and a whole lot more. Be a cowboy, cowgirl, Indian or an engineer. Shop along Main Street, learn to clog or pan for gold. Tweetsie Railroad has amusement rides for all

Cowboys, Indians and Can-Can girls are just a few of the characters from the old West roaming the frontier town of Tweetsie Junction.

ages and live entertainment throughout the park. Ride the chair lift to Miner's Mountain, and enjoy the deer and goats in The Deer Park. And of course, hop aboard our historic train for a fun-filled three-mile Wild West journey through the scenic mountains.

Enjoy a scenic train ride through the mountains.

Traveler info:
Exit: MP 291, Boone Exit
♿ FAX

Open: Fri., Sat., Sun. in May. Seven days a week from Memorial Day thru mid-Aug. Fri., Sat., Sun. from mid-Aug. thru Oct.
Admission: $26 adults; $18 children (ages 3-12)
For more info:
Tweetsie Railroad
U.S. 321
Blowing Rock, NC 28605
(800) 526-5740
(828) 264-9061
www.tweetsie.com

❻ b *Please refer to map*

Blowing Rock Park contains an observation tower, nature walk and small garden waterfall.

www.blowingrock.com
•From MP 291.9, Hwy. 321S
•The Only Full-Service Town Directly on the Parkway

Blowing Rock (elevation 4,000 feet) sits astride the Eastern Continental Divide. Try a walking tour of historic buildings or enjoy the arts. Summer home of the N.C. Symphony, the town has professional summer stock theater plus arts and crafts shows called "Art in the Park." Head south on U.S. 321 to visit the village's namesake, **The Blowing Rock**, an immense cliff, 4,000 feet above sea level, overhanging the Johns River Gorge. A unique phenomenon gave the rock its name. The rock walls of the gorge form a flume through which the northwest wind sweeps with such force that it returns light objects (such as handkerchiefs) thrown over the edge from the rock.

Tweetsie Railroad **6** B

U.S. 321
Blowing Rock, NC 28605
(800) 526-5740
(828) 264-9061
www.tweetsie.com
•Exit at MP 291, Boone Exit
•The Tweetsie locomotive was once owned by Gene Autry

The historic Tweetsie train takes passengers on an excursion through the mountains. But the trip is not peaceful; there are train robbers lurking around the bend. Tour the Wild West

Boone CVB

Four Real Seasons

Boone, NC – three thousand feet closer to heaven, the views are longer, and life is slower.

Within a few miles of Boone are seven golf courses, and over 400 artists drawing inspiration from the majesty of the mountains.

Go biking, rock climbing, fishing or rafting. Even ski in the winter! Outfitters can supply everything you need.

Call for more details on events, attractions and lodging in the High Country.

Views are longer in Boone.

Traveler info:
Distance: Approx. 5 miles from Parkway
For more info:
Boone Convention and Visitor Bureau
208 Howard St.
Boone, NC 28607
(800) 852-9506
(828) 262-3516
info@visitBooneNC.com
www.visitbooneNC.com

5 *Please refer to map*

DeWoolfson Down

America's Finest Quality Since 1982

DeWoolfson Down is a nationally recognized manufacturer of America's finest quality down comforters, pillows and featherbeds. Since 1982 their products have been made in the North Carolina High Country and offered to local residents and travelers who visit their original store, located on Highway 105, between Boone and Linville, NC. While most large-scale production is now done at DeWoolfson's nearby plant, visitors to the store are still treated to a short tour of their unique down workshop to learn how their products are made.

Stop by and see how special their comforters and pillows really are.

Traveler info:
Distance: 10 miles from Parkway
Open: Mon.-Sat. 9am-5pm; Sun. 12pm-5pm June - Oct.
For more info:
DeWoolfson Down
9452 Hwy. 105
Banner Elk, NC 28604
(800) 833-3696
www.dewoolfsondown.com

9 *Please refer to map*

A beloved part of the Valle Crucis community, the Mast General Store has been open since 1883, and is still a working store today.

town, shop on Main Street, hike up Miner's Mountain to pan for gold, visit Deer Park petting zoo and end the day with a musical show. Open May-October. For more information see box on page 68.

Valle Crucis/   ❼ Mast General Store

Hwy. 194
Valle Crucis, NC 28691
(828) 963-6511
info@mastgeneralstore.com
www.mastgeneralstore.com
• At either MP 291.9 or MP 305.2, take U.S. 221, N.C. 105, then N.C. 194
• An 1883 general store in the state's first rural historic district

Opened in 1883, Mast General Store offered "Quality goods for the living, coffins & caskets for the dead." You can still shop the mercantile for everything from stone-ground meal to lye soap plus 500 old-fashioned candies to tempt you. On-site pottery demos are

---

Mast General Store

Nestled in a Beautiful Mountain Valley

Discover why the National Historic Register calls Mast General Store "One of the best remaining examples of an old country store." This venerable landmark in Valle Crucis - a community on the National Register of Historic Places - has featured quality goods, traditional clothing, outdoor

Young and old enjoy bottlecap checkers by Mast Store's vintage potbellied stove.

❼ a   Please refer to map

Charles Kuralt called the Mast Store "a destination" and the "Soul of the South."

gear, and rugged footwear since 1883.

Once known for selling everything from "cradles to caskets" you can still mail a letter at the corner post office or sip a nickel cup of coffee by the pot bellied stove. Here you'll also find the Mast Annex (c.1909) offering a unique blend of outdoor gear, clothing and candy. Also visit Mast's Old Boone Mercantile (c.1913) a vintage emporium in

nearby Boone as well as restored mercantiles in Asheville, Waynesville and Hendersonville, NC and now Greeneville, SC.

Traveler info:
Exit: MP 292
For more info:
Mast General Store
Hwy. 194
Valle Crucis, NC 28691
(828) 963-6511
www.mastgeneralstore.com
www.maststoreonline.com

conducted at the Little Red School House behind the store; the nearby 1909 Annex is a complete mountain outfitter. See page 70 for more information.

Beech Mountain ⑧

At more than 5,500 feet Beech Mountain is the highest ski area in eastern North America.

NORMAN POOLE

Beech Mountain Chamber of Commerce
403A Beech Mountain Pkwy.
Beech Mountain,
NC 28604
(800) 468-5506
(828) 387-9283
chamber@beechmtn.com
www.beechmtn.com
•MP 305.2, take U.S. 221, N.C. 105 & then N.C. 184
•"Eastern America's Highest Incorporated Town"

At 5,506 feet, the resort community of Beech Mountain is home to **Ski Beech**, where the skiing season lasts from mid-Nov.-mid-March. Features include 15 trails, slopes of varying difficulty, lighted nighttime skiing,

ice skating and an alpine village. (800) 438-2093, www.skibeech.com. Other seasons bring biking, horseback riding, fishing and whitewater. See box below for more information.

Grandfather Mountain ⑩

Linville, NC 28646
(828) 733-4337,

(800) 468-7325
nature@grandfather.com
www.grandfather.com
•U.S. 221, 1 mile south of MP 305 or 2 miles north of Linville, N.C.
•The highest point in the Blue Ridge Mountains at 5,964 feet

Grandfather Mountain is generally known for its mile-high swinging bridge. The 228-foot suspension bridge spans an 80-foot

Elevate Yourself! Beech Mountain, NC

Eastern America's Highest Town

Just around the corner from your everyday routine, you'll find a one-stop mountain getaway with a welcoming atmosphere, cultural charm, and recreation for every season.

Cresting above 5,500 ft., Beech Mountain features great skiing, sledding, skating, and winter activities

Skiers and snowboarders of all ages and skill levels enjoy the east's premier winter resort.

Recreational opportunities and spectacular views abound during the summer months.

for the whole family.

In the summer, hiking, golf, and mountain biking thrive at Beech, where temperatures rarely exceed 70 degrees. Fall finds the mountainsides draped with brilliant colors - a perfect backdrop for street dances, art exhibitions and live music.

At Beech, you'll be treated like a friend from the moment you arrive. It's our way of making sure your stay is as enjoyable as

it can possibly be. So head on up Beech Mountain - your good spirits will thank you later.

Traveler info:
Exit: 12 miles from Parkway
For more info:
Beech Mountain COC
403-A Beech Mountain Pkwy.
Beech Mountain, NC 28604
(800) 468-5506
chamber@beechmtn.com
www.beechmtn.com

⑧ Please refer to map

Grandfather Mountain

Discover Nature on a Whole Different Level

The highest peak in the Blue Ridge welcomes guests with easy access to its rugged heights and spectacular vistas. Cross the famous Mile High Swinging Bridge and take in 360-degree views from a mile above sea level.

Photograph bears, cougars, eagles and otters in their natural habitats. Explore the Nature Museum, dine in the restaurant, or picnic surrounded by nature. Stroll down gentle nature trails or traverse the high peaks on the South's best alpine trails.

Traveler info:
Exit: MP 305

10 *Please refer to map*

Feel like you are standing on top of the world.

 ♿ FAX
Open: 8am-5pm in winter, 8am-6pm in spring and fall, 8am-7pm in summer
Admission: Children 4-12 $6, Adults 13-59 $12, Seniors 60+ $11
For more info:
Grandfather Mountain
PO Box 129
Linville, NC 28646
(800) 468-7325
www.grandfather.com

HUGH MORTON / COURTESY GRANDFATHER MOUNTAIN

Mountain ridges retreat for dozens of miles in all directions from the top of Grandfather Mountain.

chasm. But there's so much more to this true jewel of the Blue Ridge. Grandfather Mountain is considered the most biologically diverse mountain in the eastern United States and is the only private park designated by the United Nations as an International Biosphere Reserve – a place where humans and nature can thrive in harmony. See box at left for more information.

Linville Gorge Wilderness ⓫

Pisgah National Forest, Grandfather Ranger District, Rt. 1, Box 110-A
Nebo, NC 28761
(828) 652-2144
www.cs.unca.edu/nfsnc
•MP 315
•Linville Gorge, called the Grand Canyon of the South

Linville Gorge Wilderness is 12,000 acres of wild land with plenty of wildlife. Unique rock formations include Sitting Bear, Table Rock and the Chimneys. The gorge is a 12-mile-long, 1,500-foot-deep gash cut by the Linville River. **Linville Falls**, a series of two falls, plunges into the gorge. Enjoy the hiking trails; camping is permitted.

Switzerland Inn

Get Away from the Ordinary

Since 1910 the Switzerland Inn has offered a unique experience to the traveler seeking something out of the ordinary. Tucked away in the mountains of western North Carolina, it is one of the finest Inns in the Southeast. Our cottages give you the flavor of the mountains, and they offer a higher level of privacy. The rooms in the Main Lodge beckon you to the Swiss Alps with their hand-painted murals and rich-toned wainscoting. Room rates are $95-$180 per night, depending on unit and season.

Gaze at one of the most magnificent mountain views in the region.

Traveler info:
Exit: MP 334
For more info:
Switzerland Inn
PO Box 399
Little Switzerland, NC 28749
(800) 654-4026
(828) 765-2153
www.switzerlandinn.com

14 *Please refer to map*

Experience the beauty of a natural limestone cavern at Linville Caverns.

RONNIE LUTTRELL

Linville Gorge is one of the deepest east of the Mississippi; it's reached near MP 316.3

Linville Caverns

An Underground Adventure Awaits

Venture a few miles off the Parkway for a unique view of nature at work "inside" the mountains! Guided tours of Humpback Mountain allow visitors to walk beside an underground stream full of blind trout, get a close-up view of stalactites and stalagmites, see our vivid mineral colors, peer into our "Bottomless Pool", learn about other forms of life underground, and even experience total darkness!

Traveler info:
Distance: 4 miles from Parkway
Open: Daily March-Nov.; Dec., Jan., Feb. weekends only
Admission: $5 Adult, $3 Kids ages 5-12
For more info:
Linville Caverns
PO Box 567
Marion, NC 28752
(828) 756-4171
(800) 419-0540
www.linvillecaverns.com

Linville Caverns 🄬

U.S. 221
Marion, NC 28752
(800) 419-0540
(828) 756-4171
cavetwin@wnclink.com

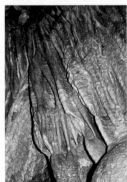

Linville Caverns offers tours from March through November.

www.linvillecaverns.com
•Exit MP 317.4 (Linville Falls Village) and left on U.S. 221
•Annual Temperature: 52 degrees

North Carolina's only show caverns, **Linville Caverns** lay undiscovered for centuries inside Humpback Mountain until 1822 when fishermen noticed trout swimming in and out of the mountain. Visitors today can view the limestone cavern as it continues to grow and create new formations. Guided tours may include a glimpse of an Eastern Pipistrelle bat hanging from the ceiling. Open March-Nov. daily, Dec.-Feb. weekends.

See box to right for more information.

🄬 *Please refer to map*

DEBORAH R. HUSO

The Orchard at Altapass was a post-retirement dream-come-true for Bill and Judy Carson when the 135-acre orchard came up for sale.

Altapass Orchard ⓭

PO Box 245
Little Switzerland, NC 28749
(888) 765-9531
billcarson@altapassorchard.com
www.altapassorchard.com
•MP 328.3 at Orchard Road, Near Spruce Pine
•Said to be the oldest continuously operating orchard in the state

A century ago, railroad workers planted several hundred acres of apple trees at Altapass. Split in half by the new Blue Ridge Parkway, only the southern half still has orchards today and is said to be the oldest continuously operating orchard in the state. You can buy apples at Altapass or follow train tracks through two tunnels that border the orchard. Tour the butterfly garden, picnic at the covered pavilion, or take a hayride. Music weekends and guided nature tours are also popular. Open seasonally, Memorial Day through October.

HIGH COUNTRY SERVICES

HISTORIC TODD GENERAL STORE

Distance: MP 276.4; three miles west on 421, turn right onto Brownwood Rd. • 3866 Railroad Grade Rd. • Todd, NC 28684 • (336) 877-1067

Come and see what all the fuss is about. Music jams on Fridays and Storytelling Tuesday evenings. Great food, antiques, authors, artists, mountain crafts. Saturday concerts feature National banjo champs. On the New River and VA Creeper Bike Trail.

www.toddgeneralstore.com

CABINS ON LAUREL CREEK

Distance: 1 mile off Parkway, near MP 249 • Laurel Springs, NC 28644 • (336) 207-7677 • Rates: $90 - $105 per night

Nestled among rolling meadows the three cabins offer a peaceful escape from everyday life. New, cozy, spotless, with dishes and linen provided. Grouped together, they are perfect for families yet offer privacy. Two cabins are pet friendly.

www.cabinsonlaurelcreek.com

www.bestwestern.com/eldrethinnatmtjefferson

BEST WESTERN ELDRETH INN

Distance: Approx. 11 miles from Parkway • PO Box 12 • 829 E. Main St. • Jefferson, NC 28640 • (800) 221-8802 • (336) 246-8845 • 48 rooms • Rates: $55 and up • AE, DC, MC, V

Experience comfortable, country hospitality. Relax in a rocking chair on the balcony. Explore Fresco Churches, Ashe Country Cheese, golf courses, Mt. Jefferson State Park and local craft shops.

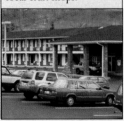

www.doeridgepottery.com

DOE RIDGE POTTERY

Distance: Approx. 8 miles from Parkway • 137 W. King St. • Boone, NC 28607 • (828) 264-1127 • E-mail: meier@doeridgepottery.com • Open: Mon.-Sat. 10am-6pm • DC, MC, V

Fine handmade stoneware pottery, inspired by my home in the Blue Ridge Mountains. Custom commission for dinnerware, lamps and other interior decor, including wedding registries, are available. Pieces are oven, food, microwave, and dishwasher safe.

HIGH COUNTRY SERVICES

FOSCOE REALTY RENTALS

Distance: 10 miles from Parkway • 133 Echota Pkwy. • Boone, NC 28607 • (800) 723-7341 • (828) 963-8142 • Rates: call for information • AE, DC, MC, V

Experience the tranquility and hospitality of the High Country from a resort getaway, minutes from Boone, Banner Elk and Blowing Rock. Each property is fully furnished and equipped, many with mountain views, hot tubs, fireplaces, and more.

www.FoscoeRentals.com

---

www.highlandsatsugar.com

THE HIGHLANDS AT SUGAR

Distance: Approx. 10 miles from Parkway • 2173 Sugar Mtn. Dr. • Banner Elk, NC 28604 • (828) 898-9601 • E-mail: highlandrsv @skybest.com • 57 rooms • Open: 8:30am - 5:30pm • AE, DC, MC, V

Our spacious one and two bedroom suites feature a large jacuzzi, a mountain stone fireplace, cable TV, and a fully equipped kitchen. Most units have a wet bar. Many resort amenities within walking distance.

INN AT YONAHLOSSEE RESORT

Distance: 2-1/2 miles from Parkway• 226 Oakley Green • Boone, NC 28607 • (800) 962-1986 • (828) 963-6400• E-mail: info@yonahlossee.com • Seasonal Rates • MC, V

Romantic inn rooms, cozy cottages and luxurious homes. Indoor and outdoor tennis, indoor pool and two fitness centers, plus conciege service. Close to hiking, skiing and horseback riding. Fine dining at the Gamekeeper Restaurant.

www.yonahlossee.com

MEADOWBROOK INN AND CIAO BELLO! RESTAURANT

Distance: 1 mile from Parkway• 711 Main St. • Blowing Rock, NC 28605 • (800) 456-5456 • Open: year-round • Rooms: 61 • ♿

Just off the Blue Ridge Parkway on historic Main Street in Blowing Rock, sits the beautiful Meadowbrook Inn. Our brook, waterfall and duck ponds set the stage for relaxing and adventure for the whole family. An indoor pool and suites - all close to shopping.

www.meadowbrook-inn.com

---

www.sugarmountain.com

SUGAR SKI AND COUNTRY CLUB

Distance: Approx. 10 miles from Parkway • 100 Sugar Ski Dr. • Banner Elk, NC 28604 • (800) 634-1320 • (828) 898-9784 • E-mail: sugarski@skybest.com

Mountaintop slopeside accommodations on Sugar Mountain. Great winter skiing, cool summer breezes. Each condominium is individual in taste and style, and all units have a fireplace, fully equipped kitchen, cable TV and telephone.

✈ Virtual Blue Ridge

VIRTUAL BLUE RIDGE

PO Box 1157 • Boone, NC 28607 • (828) 265-4026 • E-mail: info@virtualblueridge.com

Virtual Blue Ridge is the premiere online resource designed to aid you in preparing for your vacation to the Blue Ridge Parkway. Web site features include an up-to-date photo journal, travel and accommodations directory, calendar of events, complete virtual tour, news service and more.

www.virtualblueridge.com

North Carolina's Blue Ridge/Asheville

Parkway MP 312 to 423
Asheville • Black Mountain • Hendersonville •
Mount Pisgah • Lake Lure • Brevard • Hot Springs

The Paris of the South – Asheville – serves as a perfect anchor point for exploring an area rich in mountain culture and beauty. From the majesty of the Biltmore Estate to the shop-lined main streets of the region's small towns, this is an area full of surprises.

The Blue Ridge/Asheville region is a study in contrasts. The 250-room chateau called Biltmore has drawn millions to see its opulent splendor in Asheville. But many have also climbed Mount Pisgah to see a natural splendor that can be found nowhere else. Superlatives abound here: the highest mountain in the East, the loftiest waterfall, the largest private dwelling and North Carolina's state theatre. The parkway climbs many mountains and plunges through deep woods here; it is never a dull ride. The arts and crafts of the mountains are alive and well here, both in places such as the Folk Art Center where they are collected, but also out along the rural highways of the region, where practitioners carry out the crafts of centuries past. Here too are sumptuous resorts and fine restaurants, great golf and hiking and pockets of history that include the birthplace of American forestry and the homes of author Thomas Wolfe and of poet and historian Carl Sandburg.

STEPHEN SCHOOF

The brilliant purples of phlox reflect the sunset at Craggy Gardens, Blue Ridge Parkway milepost 360.

◁ *The views from the top of Chimney Rock can stretch for up to 75 miles, and includes looks at Hickory Nut Gorge and Lake Lure.*

The North Carolina Arboretum, southwest
of Asheville near MP 393, offers 426
acres of beauty and information as well as
walking tours.

Getting Around

South from Parkway MP 312, travelers reach N.C. 226, an access to I-
40, at MP 331. N.C. 80 crosses at MP
344, providing a sinuous route north to
U.S. 19E, Spruce Pine and Burnsville,
or south to I-40, Old Fort and Black
Mountain.

Near Asheville (MP 383-394),
the Parkway intersects U.S. 70,
which eventually becomes U.S.
25/70, a Scenic Byway, to Hot
Springs. Black Mountain is
10 miles east on U.S. 70,
and Chimney Rock and
Lake Lure lie 17 miles
east on U.S. 74A, another
Scenic Byway. Take U.S. 25
or N.C. 191 south for a 30-
minute drive to Hendersonville
or a slightly longer trip to Brevard
via N.C. 280.

Beyond Asheville, the Parkway
doesn't touch another major road
until MP 412, where Scenic Byway U.S.
276 drops 18 miles to Brevard.

• Revolutionary Loyalist William Mills, the first
white settler in present-day Henderson County,
was left for dead at the Battle of Kings Mountain
in 1781; he escaped a possible hanging in a
cave in Sugar Loaf Mountain and later named
Mills River, Mills Gap and Bald Top.

Key

▬	Blue Ridge Parkway
▬	Skyline Drive
▬	Highways
—	Secondary Roads
▬	Rivers/Lakes
▲	Overlooks
⋰	Tunnels
MP	Mileposts
🂠	Gasoline
♦♦	Restrooms
❙❙❙	Food
⊼	Picnicking
♦	Visitor Center
♣	State Park

The mountain backdrops
make golf in the
Asheville region extra
enjoyable.

COURTESY NC TOURISM

Mt. Mitchell Tops the Blacks' Tall Reach

Which Appalachian peak is highest? The prize goes to 6,684-foot Mt. Mitchell in North Carolina's lofty Black Mountains, just 5 miles from Parkway MP 355. The Blacks' elevations pull Canadian forests south. Here are red spruce and Fraser fir, New England cottontails and northern flying squirrels. Summer highs rarely top 75°. Sixty miles of hiking and horse trails penetrate the Blacks, which total 16 peaks over 6,000 feet.

STEPHEN SCHOOF

The view is toward the Pinnacle at sunrise, from Potato Knob in the Black Mountains.

SIGHTS AND SITES AT A GLANCE

❶ South Mountains State Park
❷ Lake James State Park
❸ Rutherford County
❹ Crabtree Meadows Café and Gift Store (p. 5)
❺ Chimney Rock Park
❻ Fairfield Mountains Resort
❼ Lake Lure
　❼ᴀ Fox Run Townhouses & Fairways of the Mountains
　❼ʙ Lake Lure Tours, Marina & Beach
　❼ᴄ Premier Properties

❽ Hendersonville/Flat Rock
　❽ᴀ Mill House Lodge
❾ Flat Rock Playhouse
❿ Mt. Mitchell State Park
⓫ Black Mountain
⓬ Asheville
　⓬ᴀ Biltmore Estate
　⓬ʙ Grove Park Inn
　⓬ᴄ HandMade in America
　⓬ᴅ Haywood Park Hotel
　⓬ᴇ Inn on Biltmore Estate
　⓬ꜰ Southern Highland Craft Guild/Folk Art Center

　⓬ɢ Thomas Wolfe Memorial
　⓬ʜ Western N.C. Nature Center
⓭ Hot Springs
⓮ Mt. Pisgah
⓯ Cradle of Forestry in America
⓰ Brevard Music Festival at the Brevard Music Center

See also:
Traveler Services p. 93
Trip Planner Listing p.130

🌳 For specific locations of state parks see www.ils.unc.edu/parkproject/ncparks.html or call (919) 733-4181.

North Carolina's Whitewater Falls is often listed as the highest in the Eastern U.S., with two levels that combine for a 411-foot drop.

STEPHEN SCHOOF

Head For the Woods!

Three major Parkway attractions, two national forests, three state parks and one major river make the Blue Ridge/Asheville region a perfect place to head for the woods.

At MP 339 is the 253-acre **Crabtree Meadows** complex, where a moderate 2.5-mile trail descends to an 80-foot cascade on Crabtree Creek.

Gravel FR-472 junctions at MP 352, descending to trails, a campground and prime fishing spots. Down the road, Carolina Hemlocks Recreation Area boasts the popular South Toe swimming hole.

Mount Mitchell State Park appears at MP 355. Nestled in 18,000 acres of Pisgah National Forest and Parkway properties, this chunk of the Black Mountains is a hub for backpackers exploring the area's

6,000-foot peaks.

Other state parks in the region include Lake James State Park in McDowell County, where the impounded Linville and Catawba rivers form a 6,510-acre lake open to canoes and motorcraft, and much wilder **South Mountains State Park** in Burke

County, which offers 32 miles of trails through 7,400 acres of forests, with 80-foot High Shoals Falls the main draw.

On the Parkway again, MP 364 marks the 5,500-foot series of heath balds topping the Great Craggy Mountains north of Asheville. Trails ascend Craggy Pinnacle and **Craggy Gardens**, where Catawba rhododendrons bloom in June.

At MP 408, there's a 1.5-mile hike to 5,721-foot Mt. Pisgah. Its southeastern flanks lead into Pisgah National Forest's Pisgah District, where a network of trails connects creeks, waterfalls, sharp peaks and occasional granite domes for hikers, bikers, horseback riders, tubers and climbers. Farther south in Nantahala National Forest are trails around 411-foot **Whitewater Falls** and the Horsepasture

The Appalachian Trail parallels the Parkway in many areas.

LEN HOLLAND

River, which includes five waterfalls in a less-than-two-mile stretch.

Pisgah's Appalachian/ French Broad District in Madison County offers 70 miles of the Appalachian Trail, plus shorter trips into gorges. Here also is the heart of whitewater rafting, with outfitters along the French Broad River offering class III and IV rapids, or gentler family float trips.

•Pisgah and Nantahala
National Forests
US Forest Service
PO Box 2750
Asheville, NC 28802
(828) 257-4200
mailroom_r8_north_carolina@
fs.fed.us
www.cs.unca.edu/nfsnc

•South Mountains
State Park ❶
3001 South Mountains
State Park Ave.
Connelly Springs, NC 28612
(828) 433-4772
south.mountains@ncmail.net
www.ils.unc.edu/parkproject/
visit/somo/home.html

Hendersonville's downtown is full of charm.

Lake James State Park ❷

Hwy. 126
P.O. Box 340
Nebo, NC 28761
(828) 652-5047
lake.james@ncmail.net
www.ils.unc.edu/parkproject/
visit/laja/home.html

•Lake James has more than 150 miles of shoreline

Tucked away at the base of Linville Gorge, Lake James is a 6,510-acre lake in one of the state's newest parks. The park occupies about 595 acres on the lake's southern shore. Swim-

---

Gems in the NC Blue Ridge Mountain Foothills

Lake Lure, Chimney Rock and Quaint Downtowns

Hop off the Parkway at MP 317.55, follow U.S. 221 S., crossing I-40. Travel 20 miles, and you will find yourself on the quaint main street of Rutherfordton. Antique shops, cozy restaurants alive with friendly conversation and specialty stores await you. Or, you can stay

Have a day in the sun at Lake Lure Beach.

on the Parkway and exit at MP 384. Follow the Bat Cave signs on Hwy. 74 and enter the Villages of Chimney Rock and Lake Lure. Picturesque Rocky Broad River leads you through these small villages. A glimpse skyward is Chimney Rock Park, a movie site for *The Last of the Mohicans*. Around the bend is beautiful Lake Lure,

the site of yet another movie filming, *Dirty Dancing*.

Traveler info:
Exit: MP 317.55
For more info:
Rutherford County Tourism
1990 U.S. Hwy. 221 S.
Forest City, NC 28043
(800) 849-5998
(828) 245-1492
www.rutherfordtourism.com

Journey through the small towns and scenic byways to find a myriad of things to do.

❸ *Please refer to map*

Chimney Rock Park

More Than A Rock, It's A Mountain of Possibilities!

Reach the top of a mountain near Asheville in about 30 seconds. That's the time it takes to ride the 26 story elevator built inside the magnificent Chimney Rock. But, that's only the beginning. You can take a leisurely stroll, a challenging hike, or do something fun with the kids on the Great Woodland Adventure. With the Park's towering cliffs, lush woods and 404-foot waterfall, there's no shortage of ways to find yourself breathless.

Savor a 75-mile view of Lake Lure and Hickory Nut Gorge from atop the "Rock".

Hours: Open daily year-round (weather permitting); except Christmas and New Year's Day. 8:30am-4:30pm EST; 8:30am-5:30pm DST.
Open: 1-1/2 hours after Ticket Plaza closes
For more info:
Chimney Rock Park
HWY. 64/74A
Chimney Rock, NC 28720
(800) 277-9611
www.chimneyrockpark.com

Traveler info:
Exit: MP 384.7; 20 miles from Parkway

⑤ *Please refer to map*

COURTESY NC TOURISM

Chimney Rock just 315 feet fror

ming, picnicking, boating, water-skiing and fishing are popular here. There are 20 walk-to campsites plus hiking trails with lake overlooks.

Chimney Rock Park **❺**

Highway 64/74A
PO Box 39
Chimney Rock, NC 28720
(800) 277-9611
visit@chimneyrockpark.com
www.chimneyrockpark.com
•Located on US 64/74A, 25 miles southeast of Asheville
•The Chimney is a 500-million year old rock

With 75-mile views, unusual rock formations and the 404-foot Hickory Nut Falls, this park has plenty of breathtaking sights. Four trails lead to the falls; trail specialists can answer your questions. Climb stairs and bridges or take a 26-story elevator to reach the Chimney level. The family-owned park has a nature center, picnic area and plenty of opportunities for bird-watching. The "Opera Box," a slab of gneiss broken along a foliation plane, overlooks Lake Lure. Inspiration Point provides rare views of Lake Lure and Hickory Nut Falls together. See box on page 82 for more information.

Fairfield Mountains

Let's Talk Resort

Lakeside magic. Here in the foothills of the Blue Ridge Mountains lies an area, a truly first class resort, located in the unique year round comfort of the isothermal belt where winter is warmer, summer is longer and fall is brilliant. A true four-season resort with golf, tennis, indoor and outdoor pools, sauna, hiking, and two 18-hole championship golf courses, plus "Tee for Two" golf packages that include accommodations, cart and green fees. Choose from intimate lakefront dining or prepare meals in your own kitchen. Come visit and be renewed.

Enjoy golfing at either Apple Valley Country Club or Bald Mountain Golf Club.

Traveler info:
Exit: MP 384.7
For more info:
Fairfield Mountain Resort
747 Buffalo Creek Rd.
Lake Lure, NC 28746
(800) 829-3149
(828) 625-9111
www.fairfieldmountains.com

⑥ *Please refer to map*

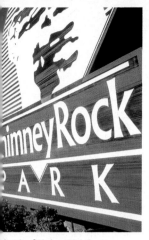

h side of Hickory Nut Gorge.

Lake Lure ❼

U.S. 64-74A
Lake Lure
(828) 625-0077
(877) FUN-4-ALL
www.lakelure.com

Experience firsthand the unique beauty of Lake Lure from the comfort of a luxurious seat aboard one of the spacious covered tour boats. See locations for blockbuster film "Dirty Dancing." See acres and acres of unsurpassed natural beauty, wildlife and legend. Admission charged.

Hendersonville ❽

•Hendersonville County Travel and Tourism
201 S. Main St.
Hendersonville, NC 28792
(828) 693-9708
(800) 828-4244
www.historichendersonville.org

Forty minutes south on I-26 is Hendersonville, population 7,000. In the heart of North Carolina's apple industry, the 150-year-old town offers its Apple Festival every Labor Day. Rated one of the country's 100 best small towns, Hendersonville is also one of the top 20 retirement meccas in the United States. Its downtown holds 180 businesses, including galleries, cafes and ice cream parlors.

Lake Lure Tours, Marina and Beach

Dive Into Beautiful Lake Lure

Step aboard our luxurious pontoon boats and discover spectacular Lake Lure. Scenic one-hour boat tours, champagne, twilight and dinner cruises. Canoe, kayak, paddle boat, electric boat and pontoon rentals, too. Splash at the beach and water park.

Scenic boat tours are just one of the many activities in magnificent Lake Lure.

Traveler info:
Distance: Approx. 22 miles from Parkway
& FAX
Open: Hours vary by season and facility

For more info:
Lake Lure Tours
PO Box 541
Lake Lure, NC 28746
(877) FUN-4-ALL (386-4255)
(828) 625-1373
E-mail: skipper@lakelure.com
www.lakelure.com

❼ B *Please refer to map*

Premier Properties Lake Country Real Estate

Lake, Resort and Mountain Sales and Rentals

Enjoy majestic mountains, a pristine lake, or the waters of an old noble river from the deck of your own private vacation rental home. From a romantic getaway to a special family gathering - we offer accommodations to fit every taste and budget. Enjoy water sports, hiking and golf, or venture out within an hours drive to take pleasure in some of the best attractions and recreation the region has to offer. Make your reservations today.

Rustic to elegant and everything in between.

Traveler info:
Exit: 25 miles from Parkway
Open: Year-round
For more info:
Premier Properties
2992 Memorial Hwy.
Lake Lure, NC 28746
(800) 742-9556
(888) 625-9600
www.LakeCountryNC.com/brpg

❼ C *Please refer to map*

Mt. Mitchell takes its name from Elisha Mitchell, the man who fell to his death while exploring it.

play, and for the last 50 years North Carolina's State Theater has held almost 400 shows in its rustic barn-style building. This "summer" theater seats 458 patrons and holds performances from mid-May to mid-December, using its own Vagabond Players as well as guest actors.

The playhouse features three free productions relating to writer/poet Carl Sandburg, who used to spend evenings here playing music. Held weekly June through August, these appear on-location at Connemara, Carl Sandburg's former home – now a National Historic Site – just across the street.

Flat Rock Playhouse ⑨

2661 Greenville Highway
Flat Rock, NC 28731
(828) 693-0731
frp@flatrockplayhouse.org
www.flatrockplayhouse.org

•Rated one of the top 10 summer theaters in the U.S.

The woodsy community of Flat Rock is a surprisingly wonderful place to catch a professional production of a Broadway

Mount Mitchell State Park ⑩

2388 State Hwy. 128
Burnsville, NC 28714
(828) 675-4611

FLAT ROCK PLAYHOUSE

*Flat Rock Playhouse offers
professional theater productions.*

mount.mitchell@ncmail.net
www.ils.unc.edu/parkproject/
visit/momi/home.html
•MP 355, then Hwy. 128
•Temperatures rarely pass 75
degrees here in summer

Soaring more than a mile
high (6,684 feet), **Mount
Mitchell** is the highest peak
in the eastern U.S. The state
park surrounding the peak
has camping, picnicking and
hiking on trails connecting
to the **Pisgah National
Forest**. Mount Mitchell
itself is just 285 yards from
the summit parking lot.
Mount Mitchell is part of
the Black Mountains; Cana-
dian-like forests are comfortable in these mountain
elevations.

Black Mountain ⓫

Black Mountain-Swannanoa
Chamber of Commerce
201 E. State Street
Black Mountain, NC 28711
(828) 669-2300
(800) 669-2301
Fax (828) 669-1407
info@blackmountain.org
www.blackmountain.org
www.exploreblackmountain.com
•Exit MP 377
•Nicknamed the Front Porch of
Western North Carolina

An old railroad town sur-
rounded by 6,000-foot
peaks, Black Mountain has
an abundance of antique
stores, craft shops and art
galleries. Enjoy the old hard-

Black Mountain, North Carolina

Front Porch
of Western NC

*Step back in time in
Black Mountain.*

Minutes from Asheville
and years from the
21st century, visitors can
delight in the wonders of
Black Mountain. Nick-
named the "Front Porch of
Western North Carolina,"
you'll be fascinated by this
charming town!

Strolling through our
Historic District, you will
find artisans working in
their shops, antique dealers,
furniture stores, galleries
and delightful aromas from
cafes and restaurants.

Visit the old hardware
store, 1890's train depot,
"Valley Museum" or catch
a play at the "Center for
the Arts."

Traveler info:
Exit: MP 380, then East
Hwy. 70, 8 miles to Black
Mountain, NC
For more info:
Black Mountain COC
201 E. State St.
Black Mountain, NC 28711
(877) 669-2322
www.exploreblackmountain.com

11 *Please refer to map*

Your Haven:
Mill House Lodge

Casual, Unhurried
Pace of a Mountain
Retreat

Mill House Lodge is
located minutes
from Flat Rock Playhouse,
Carl Sandburg Home and
Historic Downtown
Hendersonville.
Accommodations are
available from a weekend
for two, to family reunions
or other group gatherings.
All of our guest rooms
have a kitchenette or full
kitchen as well as cable
television. Seven guest
lodges surround the pri-
vate and tranquil four-acre
lake for fishing and canoeing.

*Enjoy canoeing, fishing or a
spot to relax with nature.*

Traveler info:
Exit: 25 miles from the
Parkway
Open: Open all year
For more info:
Mill House Lodge
P.O. Box 309
Flat Rock, NC 28731
800-736-6073
www.millhouselodge.com

8 **A** *Please refer to map*

The Biltmore House, America's largest private residence, is a "must see" when near Asheville and is the anchor attraction of the estate.

ware store, 1890s refurbished train depot brimming with antiques, collection of unique eateries and wide choice of accommodations. You can even enjoy a hand-dipped cone at the corner ice cream parlor. See box on page 85 for more information.

Asheville 🔟

Asheville Convention & Visitors Bureau
151 Haywood St.
Asheville, NC 28801
(828) 258-6101
(888) 247-9811
visit@exploreasheville.com
www.exploreasheville.com
•MP 380
•Called the "Paris of the South"

Choosing to visit Asheville is easy – deciding what to do is not. Choices include **Pack Place** housing five cultural institutions including **Asheville Art Museum** and **Colburn Gem & Mineral Museum**; **North Carolina Arboretum**; and the boyhood home of author **Thomas Wolfe,** the living history **Western North Carolina Nature Center**. A visit to **Biltmore Estate** is a must and a stay at the **Grove Park Inn** is a dream. The AAA four-diamond resort has golf, swimming and fine dining (800) 438-5800. See box on page 87 for more information on Asheville.

Biltmore Estate 🔟ᴿ

One Lodge Street
Asheville, NC 28801
(800) 624-1575
(828) 225-1333
happenings@biltmore.com
www.biltmore.com
•Four miles north on U.S. 25 from MP 389
•Largest private dwelling in the U.S.

George Vanderbilt's 250-room chateau opened here in 1895; today, visitors still can't get enough of the estate's splendor. The tailored gardens, greenhouse and antique-filled rooms are astounding. The estate features shops, restaurants, winery and the Inn on Biltmore Estate, where guests can spend the night and rise to discover more of the beauty of the grounds the next day.

Modeled after the 16th-century chateaus of France, the 250-room mansion opened in 1895 with such novelties as electric lighting, mechanical refrigeration, central heat and indoor plumbing.

Frederick Law Olmstead, the famed designer of Central Park, was hired to plan 250 acres of landscaping, including 10 acres of formal flower gardens and a

George Vanderbilt

After building the country's largest private home, George Vanderbilt turned his 125,000-acre Biltmore Estate into a functional enterprise. From its opening in 1895, he introduced new farming techniques, managed a 90,000-square-foot dairy, and, by employing world-renowned land managers, enabled his vast properties to hold their beauty up to the present day.

George Vanderbilt

Experience Asheville, Again and Again!

Breathtaking Vistas, Majestic Mountains, and a Dynamic Culture All in One Incredible City

Rafting is only one of the activities outdoor enthusiasts can enjoy.

There's something magical and exciting to do around every corner in Asheville, North Carolina. Nestled in some of the nation's highest mountains, you'll find a special place that brings out the best in people from all walks of life. The mountain atmosphere has inspired visitors and residents alike for more than two centuries.

Artisans and craftspeople have made this beautiful city their home for years and continue their artistic traditions for a new generation. Nature lovers delight in every view along the abundant hiking trails, in the endless display of wildflowers on hillsides and in the marvelous public gardens.

Take a drive along the nation's most scenic highway, the Blue Ridge Parkway, or stroll through America's largest private home, Biltmore Estate. Enjoy the festivals, arts and crafts fairs, and take a walking tour through Asheville's historic Art Deco city.

Stare out into the sea of quiet, rolling mountains.

You'll find quaint shops, crafts and art galleries, antiques, and plenty of delectable dining. Lunch at a cozy main street café and plan the rest of your stay from there. No matter when you decide to visit our magnificent mountains, you'll find plenty to see and do in and around Asheville. From grand resort to intimate B&B, fine hotel to rustic lodge, a variety of accommodations will allow you to relax in luxury or at an out of the way spot. Special packages online. Your adventure awaits you in Asheville.

Traveler info:
Exit: MP 380
For more info:
Asheville Convention and Visitors Bureau
151 Haywood St.
Asheville, NC 28801
(800) 232-7224
www.exploreasheville.com

The city of Asheville welcomes visitors with breathtaking views.

12 *Please refer to map*

The Folk Art Center, just off the parkway at Asheville, houses the work of members of the Southern Highland Craft Guild.

•MP 382 in Asheville
•The Guild operates five retail shops representing Guild members' work

The crafts of more than 800 artisans from the Southeastern U.S. are on display at the Craft Guild, located in the Folk Art Center. Visitors may purchase crafts in the Allenstand Craft Shop and tour the 3,000-piece permanent craft collection from the early 1900s. Craft demonstrations are offered on-site daily. For more information see page 91.

Western North Carolina Nature Center ⑫ H

75 Gashes Creek Road, Asheville, NC 28805
(828) 298-5600
Fax (828) 298-2644
www.wncnaturecenter.org
•Off U.S. 70, 1.5 miles west of MP 382
•The educational farm introduces children to farm animals

This living museum in Asheville exhibits the plant and animal wildlife of the Southern Appalachians on self-guided tours. See cougar and bobcat in the Predator Habitat, southern flying squirrels in the Nocturnal Hall and playful otters in the Otter Habitat. Children and adults alike will enjoy the African pygmy goats at the petting area.

serpentine three-mile approach road. Vanderbilt also brought new farming techniques to the area, and the estate's original 90,000-square-foot dairy now houses a modern winery.

Biltmore's forestry department may have had the greatest influence. It was under Vanderbilt's employ that Carl Schenck started the country's first forestry school.

Vanderbilt's heirs now own and operate the remaining acreage, which employs 800 people and draws more than 900,000 visitors per year. Self-guided tours usually begin with the first floor's Winter Garden, a sunken marble atrium. Vanderbilt's elaborate tastes appear in the 70,000 possessions still filling the house. Outside, Olmstead's landscaping continues to inspire. The Walled Garden blooms with 50,000 tulips in spring, and the Bass Pond offers shade and falling water in the summer.

Year-round events make the Biltmore a destination for any season – from spring's Easter egg hunt and Festival of Flowers to summer's evening outdoor concerts to fall's English Harvest Fair to winter's Christmas at the Biltmore. For more information see page 90.

Folk Art Center and Southern Highland Craft Guild ⑫ F

P. O. Box 9545
Asheville, NC 28815
(828) 298-7928
Fax: (828) 298-7962
parkwaycraft@skybest.com
www.southernhighlandguild.org/folkart.html

The WNC Nature Center is a "hands-on" experience.

The Grove Park Inn Resort & Spa

Mountains. Water. Sky. Heaven.

The Grove Park Inn Resort & Spa is one of the South's most loved resorts. Its 18-hole golf course, designed by Donald Ross.

Located just 15 minutes from the Parkway, this famed resort has been charming guests with an exceptional blend of history, hospitality and panoramic views for over 90 years. The Inn's striking granite facades and carefully preserved Arts & Crafts interior have led to a listing on the National Register of Historic Places.

The Inn is home to 510 guest rooms, including a recently renovated club floor and suites boasting an assortment of themes ranging from the Fabulous 50s to Donald Ross golf and an homage to the resort's fabulous Spa.

As the resort's leading amenity and most high-profile feature, The Spa combines dramatic design - the centerpiece of which is a cavernous underground atrium with indoor waterfalls - with a host of pampering treatments, many of them Spa exclusives.

Equally world-class in design and appeal - not to mention accolades from national publications - is the resort's Donald Ross

Soak up the splendor of the surrounding Blue Ridge Mountains from one of the Spa's outdoor pools.

championship golf course.

Other recreational amenities include a state-of-the-art Sports Complex featuring racquetball, indoor and outdoor tennis, an indoor pool, a full compliment of cardio- and weight-training equipment and a variety of daily fitness classes.

The resort also offers exquisite dining at its four restaurants, along with an endless array of delights in its gallery of intriguing shops.

In all, it's easy to see how, at The Grove Park Inn Resort & Spa, mountains, water and sky add up to a feeling that's nothing short of heaven.

Traveler info:
Distance: Approx. 10 miles from Parkway
Open: Year-round
For more info:
The Grove Park Inn Resort and Spa
290 Macon Ave.
Asheville, NC 28804
(800) 438-5800
www.groveparkinn.com

Savor world-class cuisine in one of the resort's four award-winning restaurants.

12 B *Please refer to map*

Thomas Wolfe Memorial ⑫ G

52 N. Market St.
Asheville, NC 28801
(828) 253-8304
www.wolfememorial.com

Thomas Wolfe immortalized the Old Kentucky Home boarding house in

The Old Kentucky Home boarding house owned by Thomas Wolfe's mother.

COURTESY PACK LIBRARY

his book "Look Homeward, Angel" with a colorful portrayal of his family and his hometown of Asheville. The book became a literary sensation when it was published in 1929 – and, thanks to its thinly disguised portraits of dozens of Asheville residents, a hometown scandal.

For seven years following "Angel's" publication, the fire he had kindled with his words kept Tom Wolfe from going home. When he did, it was to this boarding house owned by his mother

Destroyed by a fire set by arsonists in 1998 it reopened in 2004.

Hot Springs/ Hot Springs Resort Spa ⑬

315 Bridge Street
P.O. Box 428
Hot Springs, NC 28743-0428
(828) 622-7676
(800) 462-0933

Fax: (828) 622-7615
info@nchotsprings.com
nchotsprings.com
•Take 19/23 N,
exit 25/70 N
•Hot spring water
year-round

Hot Springs is a "mountain-locked" 1,000-acre plain with peaks sheltering

 ⑫ A ⑫ E *Please refer to map*

Native Americans were the first to discover the 100-plus-degree water from which the town received its name.

it on all sides, providing a year-round temperate climate. Tourists have been drawn to the 104 degree spring waters since 1778. Guests enjoy the water in a dozen spring-fed hot tubs in a wooded area by the French Broad River where mineral water is pumped from the springs.

Mount Pisgah ⑭

(828) 298-0398
www.nps.gov/blri/pisgah.htm
Located at the peak of the Blue Ridge Parkway
•MP 408.6
•Mount Pisgah is the highest developed area along the Parkway

While building Biltmore Estate, George Vanderbilt purchased Mount Pisgah and surrounding acres in the late 1800s as a hunting retreat. The nearby 16-mile Shut-In Trail is part of his original hunting route. Hike the 1.5 mile trail to 5,721 foot Mount Pisgah and stay at Pisgah Inn which, at almost 5,000 feet, offers scenic accommodations (828) 235-8228 (Open late Mar.-Nov.1).

"Must Have" Cultural Guides for North Carolina

Mountain Backroads and Scenic Byways

For back road guides of North Carolina's mountains, you can't get any better than *The Farms, Gardens, and Countryside Trails of Western North Carolina*, and *Craft Heritage Trails of Western North Carolina*. Guidebooks retail for $19.95 each. These beautiful books lead visitors to hundreds of interesting galleries, family farms, craft studios and historic sites connected by driving trails off of the Blue Ridge Parkway.

Order the guides online or call to purchase. Handmade in America is a non-profit organization promoting craft and cul-

Order your North Carolina cultural guide today.

ture for community and economic development in western North Carolina.

For more info:
Handmade in America
P.O. Box 2089
Asheville, NC 28802
(800) 331-4154
www.handmadeinamerica.org

⑫ **c** *Please refer to map*

Folk Art Center

Southern Highland Craft Guild

Nestled among the pines and dogwoods of the Blue Ridge Parkway, yet only a few miles from I-40 and downtown Asheville, North Carolina, the Folk Art Center is home to the Southern Highland Craft Guild. The Center showcases the finest in traditional and contemporary craft of the Southern Appalachians. It houses the guild's century-old Allanstand Craft Shop, exhibitions in three galleries, a library and an auditorium. Visit our website for event listings.

Since 1980, the Blue Ridge Parkway's Folk Art Center has been home to the Southern Highland Craft Guild.

Distance: Milepost 382
Open: Jan.-Mar. 9am-5pm Daily; Apr.-Dec. 9am-6pm Daily; closed Thanksgiving, Christmas and New Year's Day
For more info:
Southern Highland Craft Guild
P.O. Box 9545
Asheville, NC 28815
(828) 298-7928
www.southernhighlandguild.org

Traveler info:
⑫ **F** *Please refer to map*

Haywood Park Hotel

Asheville's Only Boutique Hotel

There's a difference you'll feel from the moment you arrive at Haywood Park Hotel. Because here, in the heart of downtown Asheville, we've created a place that will change your view on hotel rooms. All 33 rooms and suites have been individually decorated with such details as hand-stitched bedding, Spanish Marble and handcrafted soap dishes made by local artists. Guests from around the world are drawn to its elegant charm and well-appointed, spacious accommodations.

Feel the difference in one of our sumptuous guest rooms.

Distance: Approx. 10 miles from Parkway
Open: 24 hours
For more info:
Haywood Park Hotel
One Battery Park Ave.
Asheville, NC 28801
(828) 252-2522
E-mail:
hotelsales@haywoodpark.com
www.haywoodpark.com

Traveler info:
12 **D** *Please refer to map*

Cradle of Forestry

Where Culture and Science Come Together

Nestled below the Parkway near Brevard, NC is the birthplace of forestry in America. This historic site abounds with ways to have fun while learning about the forest and Southern Appalachian culture. The Forest Discovery Center has a movie and 15-hands on exhibits, including the fire fighting helicopter simulator and a scavenger hunt. Then head outside as two paved trails put the forest at your fingertips. We offer handicapped facilities.Take a guided tour or explore on your own.

Cultural interpreters bring the past to life at the Cradle of Forestry.

Traveler info:
Exit: MP 412
Open: Daily, 9:00 am - 5:00 pm, April 16 - Nov. 6
For more info:
Cradle of Forestry
Hwy. 276 - Pisgah Hwy.
Pisgah Forest, NC 28768
(828) 877-3130
www.cradleofforestry.com

15 *Please refer to map*

Cradle of Forestry in America   **15**

1001 Pisgah Hwy.
Ranger Station
Pisgah Forest, NC 28768
(828) 877-3130
Fax: (828) 884-5823
cfaia@citcom.net
www.cradleofforestry.com
•Four miles east on U.S. 276 from MP 412
•6,500 acres of exhibits and displays

This National Historic site lies in the heart of **Pisgah National Forest** and features the Forest Discovery Center with hands-on exhibits, paved trails past cabins, a 1915 logging train, saw mill and the woods where the first forestry school in the U.S. was established. Carl Schenck established the school among the rhododendrons and streams of George Vanderbilt's Pink Beds. The German forester succeeded Gifford Pinchot as "forest manager" of Vanderbilt's vast estate, working to make abused and

Carl Schenck

Carl Schenck

Hired as "forest manager" by George Vanderbilt in 1895, German professor Carl Schenck spent 14 years overturning contemporary lumbermen's slash-and-burn mentality. Schenck not only restored much of today's Pisgah National Forest, he also founded America's first forestry school, Cradle of Forestry, introducing a new era of responsible timber management.

over-farmed holdings healthy again.

Exhibits of Schenck's work survive at the 6,500-acre Cradle. The one-mile, paved Biltmore Campus Trail visits Schenck's school building, supply house and more.

Central to the trails is the Forest Discovery Center, which features a short movie on Vanderbilt, Pinchot and Schenck, plus such kid-friendly exhibits as an underground forest burrow and a "Flying Forest Fire-Fighting Helicopter Experience."

The Cradle of Forestry celebrates the seasons and the mountains with educational hikes, historic interpreters, festival days and outdoors skills workshops. Open April through November. For more information see page 92.

The Cradle of Forestry is the birthplace of American stewardship of mountain woodlands.

COURTESY NORTH CAROLINA TOURISM

Brevard Music Festival/Music Center 🔟

Brevard Music Center
PO Box 312
1000 Probart St.
Brevard, NC 28712
(828) 862-2100
Fax: (828) 884-2036
bmc@brevardmusic.org
www.brevardmusic.org
•Downtown Brevard, 18 miles from MP 412

•More than 80 concerts each summer

For more than 60 years, more than 400 music students have arrived at Brevard Music Center each summer for learning in a special environment. Students play side-by-side with faculty and visiting professional musicians while honing their skills daily. The public can enjoy more than 80 performances during the annual festival from June to August. The campus covers 140 acres, with the open-sided Whittington-Pfohl Auditorium seating an audi-

ence of 1,800.

Brevard's small town atmosphere makes it a great destination as well, with quaint shops, eclectic restaurants and friendly people.

BLUE RIDGE/ASHEVILLE SERVICES

COMFORT SUITES - BILTMORE SQUARE MALL

MP 393.6 • 890 Brevard Rd. • Asheville, NC 28806 • (800) 622-4005 • (828) 665-4000 • 125 rooms • ♿

All studio suites with sitting area, microwaves, refrigerators, coffee makers and hairdryers. Free extended continental breakfast, Wireless HSIA, cable with HBO, pool and coin laundry. Adjacent to the mall, movie theatre, many restaurants. Two miles from parkway and six miles from historic downtown.

www.ashevillenccomfort.com

COURTESY NC TOURISM

The Brevard Music Center hosts a major music festival every summer.

North Carolina Smokies

Parkway MP 423 to 469
Bryson City • Cashiers • Cherokee • Dillsboro • Fontana Dam • Maggie Valley • Robbinsville • Waynesville

The Great Smokies loom up to the north and west of this pretty region, offering great vistas, rugged hiking and views of the restored elk. In the shadows of the peaks, small towns offer unique shopping, fine dining and cozy hostelries.

This area has long been known as the Land of the Cherokee. The living history of these Native Americans can be seen at Oconaluftee Indian Village, the written history seen at several museums and their land of history in the hazy mountains, water-carved rocks and deep valleys they called home. See the area on foot in the Great Smoky Mountains National Park, by car along the parkway or by train on the Great Smoky Mountains Railroad. The park's history, scenic drives and wildlife are enough to fill a vacation. Be sure to visit the towns that dot the region. Waynesville, Maggie Valley, Cashiers, Franklin and Dillsboro are just a few of the towns not to miss. In addition to the pretty miles of the Blue Ridge Parkway here, don't miss the Cherohala Skyway, a relatively new highway that connects the mountains of North Carolina and Tennessee.

SCOTT CROWDER

Waynesville farmers' market is one highlight of a downtown that features brick sidewalks, plantings and shops.

◁ *The parkway snakes through miles of unspoiled forests in the Great Smoky Mountains.*

The Blue Ridge Parkway's highest elevation is reached at MP 431, on Richland Balsam Mountain. A self-guiding nature trail leads through Fraser fir and red spruce.

Getting Around

The Parkway winds through the southwestern mountains of North Carolina, meeting U.S. 441 and the Great Smoky Mountains National Park. U.S. 74 takes visitors from U.S. 441 to Murphy, in the southeast corner. U.S. 64 from Murphy to Franklin and Cashiers is part of the Mountains to the Sea National Scenic Trail. U.S. 19 winds through the towns of Maggie Valley, Cherokee and Bryson City; joins U.S. 74 through the Nantahala Gorge and into Murphy. U.S. 129 links Robbinsville with U.S. 74.

KEY

▬	Blue Ridge Parkway
▬	Skyline Drive
▬	Highways
—	Secondary Roads
▬	Rivers/Lakes
●	Overlooks
☁	Tunnels
MP	Mileposts
⛽	Gasoline
👫	Restrooms
🍴	Food
⛱	Picnicking
♦	Visitor Center

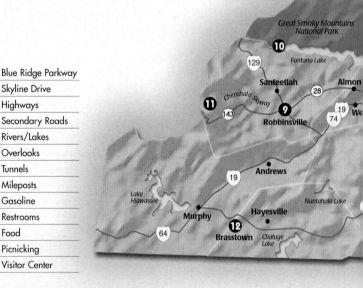

• The Nantahala Gorge, a 9-mile stretch of the Nantahala River running from Beechertown to Fontana Lake, is nationally known for its breathtaking scenery and its world-class whitewater.

• Cherokee commemorates this ancient nation in a museum, an annual outdoor drama, a re-created Indian Village and cultural events. The Cherokee were unique among the Native Americans, having a written language since the 1820s and their own newspaper by the early 1840s.

Cherokee artisans fashion crafts as their ancestors did in Oconaluftee Indian Village.

Smokies: The Most Diversity in the World

The Great Smoky Mountains National Park has the most diverse species of plant and animal life in the world. It is designated a United Nations Bio-Diversity area. More than 100 species of trees have been identified. Elevations in the Smokies range from 1,840 feet to 6,643 feet. The park encompasses 800 square miles of which 95 percent are forested. It is one of the largest protected areas in the east.

•Haywood County is home to the 6,030-foot peak that titles Charles Frazier's best-selling novel, "Cold Mountain." A total of 19 peaks in the county top 6,000'.

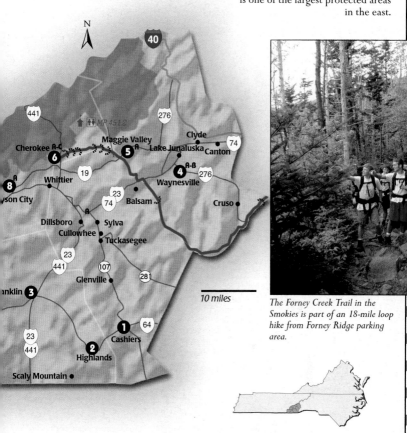

N

40

441

MP 451.2

276

Cherokee

Maggie Valley

Clyde

74

Lake Junaluska

Canton

6

5

19

4

276

8

Whittier

Waynesville

son City

23

74

Balsam

Cruso

Dillsboro

Sylva

Cullowhee

Tuckasegee

23

441

107

281

Glenville

anklin

3

10 miles

23

441

1

64

2

Cashiers

Highlands

Scaly Mountain

The Forney Creek Trail in the Smokies is part of an 18-mile loop hike from Forney Ridge parking area.

JERRY WHALEY

SIGHTS AT A GLANCE

1 Cashiers
2 Highlands Suite Hotel Mountain High Lodge
3 Franklin
4 Waynesville
  4 A Haywood County TDA
  4 B T Pennington Art Gallery
5 Maggie Valley
  5 A Great Smoky Mountains Rentals

6 Cherokee
  6 A Cherokee Indian Reservation
  6 B Harrah's Cherokee Casino
  6 c Oconaluftee
7 Great Smoky Mountains National Park
8 Bryson City
  8 A Great Smoky Mountains Railroad
9 Cherohala Skyway

10 Fontana Dam
11 Joyce Kilmer/Memorial Forest
12 John C. Campbell Folk School

See also:
Traveler Services p. 105
Trip Planner Listing p. 130

PAT & CHUCK BLACKLEY

Dry Falls, near Highlands, N.C., is one of several popular falls in the area.

With 12 gem mines to its credit, Franklin, N.C. is an excellent place to search for rubies, sapphires, amethysts, emeralds and other stones. **Franklin Gem and Mineral Museum**, in the old jail on Phillips Street, details the area's mining history. Visit **Scottish Tartans Museum & Heritage Center** to learn more of Scottish culture.

Waynesville ❹

Haywood County Tourism
Development Authority
1233 N. Main St.
Suite 1-40
Waynesville, NC 28786
(828) 452-0152
(800) 334-9036
info@smokeymountains.net
www.smokeymountains.net
•MP 443.1
•A town in the sky-3,600 feet

Waynesville is a mountain arts community. Try an eclectic walk along Main Street for gourmet coffee shops, bakeries and galleries filled with modern art. The **Museum of North Carolina Handicrafts**, 49 Shelton St., has an extensive exhibit of heritage crafts housed in the historic Shelton House. **Haywood Arts Repertory Theatre** is also housed in this 18th-century home. More information can be found in box on page 99.

Cashiers/Waterfalls ❶

Cashiers Chamber of Commerce
PO Box 238
Cashiers, NC 28717
(828) 743-5941
cashcham@dnet.net
www.cashiers-nc.com
•MP 443.1, take U.S. 23/74 to N.C. 107
•Try a Waterfall Tour

At 3,500 feet, the village of Cashiers is surrounded by peaks and waterfalls. Drive U.S. 64 from Franklin to Cashiers for views of cascading water including 250-foot-tall **Cullasaja Falls**, 11 miles east of Franklin. Walk behind the falls at **Dry Falls** on the way to Cashiers or drive your car under **Bridal Falls** nearby.

Franklin ❸

Franklin Area Chamber of Commerce

425 Porter St.
Franklin, NC 28734
(866) 372-5546
(828) 524-3161
facc@franklin-chamber.com
www.franklin-chamber.com
•MP 443.1, take U.S. 23/74 to U.S. 23/441
•The "Gem of the Smokies"

PAT & CHUCK BLACKLEY

Gem mining at Franklin involves the steps of washing and shaking down.

Maggie Valley ❺

Haywood County Tourism
Development Authority
1233 N. Main St.
Suite 1-40
Waynesville, NC 28786
(828) 452-0152
(800) 334-9036
info@smokeymountains.net
www.smokeymountains.net
•MP 443.1
•A mountain playground for all ages

Bring your camera to Maggie Valley. The almost linear town along Soco Rd (U.S.19) is a scenic drive up the valley, climbing to awesome views above the town. Enjoy snow skiing at

Maggie Valley and Waynesville, NC

Just Off the Parkway and Gateway to the Smokies

See native elk in Cataloochee Valley and enjoy a memorable family picnic.

Whether you want to get away from it all, or get right in the middle of all the action, you'll love Maggie Valley and Waynesville - Home to the real Cold Mountain and located in the heart of the Smokies.

Waynesville's downtown is filled with charm. Art galleries, antique gift shops, upscale retail and quaint eateries. Discover everything from penny candy to fine furniture.

Maggie Valley marked its 100th birthday in 2004 with its Centennial Summer celebration – a whole season of festivities including bluegrass, art shows and outhouse race! Along Soco Road, Maggie's full of fun – miniature golf, dancing, museums and even a zoo.

One of the highest, most stunning segments of the Blue Ridge Parkway curls around our southern border. Eighteen peaks in our mountains soar as high as 6,000 feet — Year-round explore the outdoors on trails, ski slopes and rivers.

Experience the great outdoors with your children – hike, camp, or ride horses in the mountains. Old fashioned swimming holes are fun for all ages.

Downtown Waynesville - enjoy our charming small towns.

Discover waterfalls, mine for gems, try whitewater rafting, fish for trout – the region makes the perfect family vacation destination.

Whatever your taste – outdoor events cater to a variety of music, dance and live theater – from bluegrass and clogging to Shakespeare and Beethoven – evenings of fun. Folkmoot, one of the Southeast's top 20 events, takes place the last two weeks of July. Maggie Valley is home to Raymond Fairchild, five time world champion banjo player who plays here many nights a year.

Evel Knieval's bike is here and so is a 1929 Dusenburg. Plus more than 250 vintage automobiles and motorcycles at Maggie Valley's newest museum – Wheels Through Time. The museum is a fascinating trip back in time with displays, photographs & memorabilia.

Traveler info:
Distance: MP 443.1
For more info:
Maggie Valley and Waynesville
1233 N. Main St.
Waynesville, NC 28786
(866) 393-4069
www.smokeymountains.net

The area offers 117 holes of spectacular mountain golf.

9 A **9** B **9** C *Please refer to map*

The Sequoyah Legacy

The Cherokee became the best educated tribe in America after Sequoyah developed a written system for the spoken language of the Cherokee. Realizing that this would be a key to development of the Cherokee Nation he came up with a graphic representation of their language. A syllabary rather than an alpha-bet, there was a symbol for each of the 86 sounds or sylla-bles) and it took 12

This illustration shows the translation of Cherokee from speech into a written system.

years to develop. In less than a year the Cherokee became the best educated tribe in America. They had a weekly newspaper; a written constitution; a Bible translation; printed stories, poems, songs and more, perserving aspects of cul-ture that might otherwise have been lost.

TPennington Art Gallery

A Unique Gallery

Teresa Pennington is a self-taught colored pencil artist who renders the scenery and land-marks of western N.C. She has just completed a third series for the Biltmore Estate and is cur-rently working on a series of Blue Ridge Parkway drawings. Teresa's trade-mark is a Pink Lady's Slipper, appearing in all her work since 1996 in memory of her mother. In her galleries you will find originals, limited edition prints, mini prints, cards and gift items. In addition, you may design your own music box choosing from a variety of artwork and tunes.

Visit the T. Pennington Art Gallery for artwork featuring western North Carolina.

Traveler info:
Distance: Approx. 5 miles from Parkway
Open: Mon.-Sat. 10am-5pm
For more info:
TPennington Art Gallery
Two Locations:
15 N. Main St.
Waynesville, NC 28786
(828) 452-9284 and
1179 Main St.
Blowing Rock, NC 28605
(828) 295-4334
tpennart@bellsouth.net
www.tpennington.com

4 **B** *Please refer to map*

Cataloochee Ski Area or visit the Old West at **Ghost Town In The Sky**. Try horseback riding at **Cat-aloochee Ranch**. **Wheels Through Time** museum dis-plays vintage motorcycles and cars. See page 99 for more information.

Cherokee　　**6**

Cherokee Visitor Center
PO Box 460
Cherokee, NC 28719
(800) 438-1601
cherokeeinfo@cherokee-nc.com
www.cherokee-nc.com
•MP 469
•The Cherokee have lived in this area over 10,000 years.

From MP 457.5 and con-tinuing through MP 469, the Blue Ridge Parkway passes through the heart of the Cherokee Indian Reser-vation in the Qualla Bound-ary. Observation points along the way give views of the Cherokee homeland.

Qualla Arts & Crafts Mutual sells authentic Cherokee-made craft items; **Museum of the Cherokee Indian** tells the Cherokee story through artifacts and high-tech exhibits. For more information see page 104.

Oconaluftee　**6**c Indian Village/ "Unto These Hills"

Drama Road off U.S. Hwy. 441 North
Cherokee Historical Assoc.
PO Box 398
Cherokee, NC 28719
(828) 497-2315, (866) 554-4557
(828)-497-2111 (off season)
cheratt@dnet.net
www.oconalufteevillage.com
•MP 469
•Learn more about Cherokee life

Tour a reconstructed 1750s Cherokee village including a seven-sided Council House at **Oconaluftee Indian Vil-lage** in Cherokee. Costumed Cherokee guides explain his-tory and culture. Native Americans demonstrate age-old arts and crafts. Open May-October.

"Unto These Hills,"

VICKIE ROZEMA

Artifacts such as this turtle shell rattle can be seen at the Museum of the Cherokee Indian.

an outdoor drama, tells the story of the Cherokee people, from Hernando DeSoto's arrival in 1540 through the 1839 Trail of Tears. Presented June 9-August 20, 2005, Mountainside Theater. Information: (866) 554-4557

Harrah's Cherokee Casino & Hotel ❻ᴮ

777 Casino Drive
Cherokee, NC 28719
(828) 497-7777
•MP 469

Harrah's Cherokee Casino brings the modern world into this protected area. See page 103 to find out more.

Great Smoky Mountain Railroad ❽ᴀ

PO Box 397
Dillsboro, NC 28725
(800) 872-4681
(828) 586-8811
traininfo@gsmr.com
www.gsmr.com
Dillsboro, Bryson City & Andrews
www.visitdillsboro.org
www.greatsmokies.com
www.andrewschambercommerce.com
•Dillsboro Depot-just past MP 443 via U.S. 74, take U.S. 441 exit south.
•Bryson Depot-via Balsam Gap or U.S. 19 from Cherokee
•See the Smokies as you chug along

Highlands Suite Hotel and Mountain High Lodge

Located on Main Street

Located in the heart of Highlands on Main Street, Highlands Suite Hotel has a casual yet very elegant atmosphere, while Mountain High Lodge is rustic and charming. Both are surrounded by the natural beauty of the North Carolina Mountains. Both hotels have numerous amenities to make you feel at home.

In the heart of Highlands, NC.

For more info:
Mountain High Lodge
200 Main St.
Highlands, NC 28741
(877) 553-4801
Highlands Suite Hotel
205 Main St.
Highlands, NC 28741
(877) 530-2835
www.mountainhighinn.com
www.highlandssuitehotel.com

Traveler info:
Distance: Approx. 55 miles from Parkway
Open: 8am-10pm In Season
Rooms: Mountain High Lodge 49; Highlands Suite Hotel 28

❷ *Please refer to map*

Great Smoky Real Estate, Inc.

Small Town Company Big on Service

From two bedrooms to larger homes, located in town or secluded - mountain views to woodsy settings - whispering streams to bold creeks.

Our homes are as individual as you are, offering fireplaces, grills, hot tubs, ping pong tables, cable/satellite, VCR/DVD and more. Pet and motorcycle friendly units are available.

With so many things to see and do in our area you can do as much or as little as you like.

Great Smoky Real Estate is here to serve all of your real estate needs from sales to rentals. Visit our web site or call our office for more information.

Walch Creekside - One of many homes we have to offer.

Traveler info:
Distance: Approximately 5 miles from the Parkway
For more info:
Great Smoky Real Estate, Inc.
PO Box 1448 /2779 Soco Rd.
Maggie Valley, NC 28751
(866) 811-4640
www.greatsmokyrentals.com

❺ ᴀ *Please refer to map*

REALTOR

JESSIE M. HARRIS

Black bear are indigeneous to the Smokies. Please don't feed them.

For a unique view of the Smoky Mountains, hop aboard the **Great Smoky Mountain Railroad** complete with 53 miles of track, 15 bridges and two tunnels. Stops along the way include **Dillsboro** for craft-shopping at **Riverwood Shops**, the state's oldest; **Bryson City** to visit **Whittier Historical Center**; and the 1890 town of **Andrews**. For more information see box below.

Great Smoky Mountains National Park ❼

National Park Headquarters
107 Park Park Headquarters Road
(865) 436-1200
GRSM_Smokies_Information@nps.gov
www.nps.gov/grsm
•MP 469

•More than 276,000 acres are in North Carolina

The Great Smoky Mountains' importance to our planet is recognized by its designation: International Biosphere Reserve. Many plants and animals here are only found in the park. The North Carolina section features **Mountain Farm Museum**, a replica mid-19th-century farm with molasses mill, blacksmith shop and 10 relocated historic buildings.

Driving tours through the park's scenic and bountiful forests and peaks are one way to explore the park. Hikers will want to try **Mount LeConte**, third highest peak in the park, for its views and challenging wilderness experiences. Bike routes, horse trails, fishing, swimming and picknicking are just a few more ways to while away the time. See page 110 for more on the Great Smoky Mountains National Park.

Great Smoky Mountains Railroad: All Aboard

Scenic Rail Excursions for All Ages

With the romance and mystique of an era gone by, guests on board the railroad will enjoy year round scenic train journeys across fertile valleys, through tunnels and across river gorges. Enjoy scenic round-trip rail excursions through the mountains of Western North Carolina. Choose from a variety of

View the colorful countryside of Western North Carolina. Photo by Michael Shermatta.

Ride behind Steam Locomotive #1702.

8 Ⓐ *Please refer to map*

half day rail excursions. New for 2005, take a ride with The Little Engine That Could in May. Spend a Day Out With Thomas™ in July or visit Santa on the Polar Express™ in December. Unique train and raft combination packages are wonderful for all ages. Experience railroading as it used to be aboard the Gourmet Dinner Train. Call for a complete schedule or visit our website.

Traveler info:
Exit: MP 443
Open: Year round
Rates: Varies based on season
For more info:
Great Smoky Mountains Railroad
119 Front St.
PO Box 397
Dillsboro, NC 28725
(800) 872-4681, Ext. BF
www.gsmr.com

Cherohala Skyway ❾

Graham County N.C. Travel
and Tourism Authority
PO Box 575
North Main Street
Robbinsville, NC 28771
(828) 479-3790
(800) 470-3790
info@GrahamCountyTravel.com
www.grahamcountytravel.com
•MP 455.7, take U.S. 19 to
N.C. 143
•Designated a North Carolina
Scenic Byway

There's plenty to see on the North Carolina side of the Cherohala Skyway, a new east-west link to Tennessee. The route looks down on the **Appalachian Mountains**, **Slickrock Wilderness** and **Joyce Kilmer Forest**. Stop along the North Carolina route at scenic pull-offs, enjoy a picnic, camp or enjoy back-country backpacking in **Citico Creek Wilderness Area**. See page 109 for more about the Cherohala Scenic Byway in Tennessee.

VICKIE ROZEMA

Cherohala Skyway, a National Scenic Highway, winds its beautiful way for 50 miles between Robbinsville, N.C. and Tellico Plains, Tenn.

Harrah's Cherokee Casino & Hotel

Four Star Quality Lodging

The Harrah's Cherokee Conference Center has everything you need to make your conference a success. Located in the heart of the beautiful Great Smoky Mountains, it's the ultimate setting for meetings, banquets, special events and more. Featuring 10,000 square feet of luxurious meeting space with

Experience the excitement of Harrah's.

up to eight individual conference rooms, our Conference Center is a perfect fit for group gatherings of any size. Because we know how important your meetings are, we even provide a dedicated Professional Planning staff working to meet your every need.

We know that the winning combination for any successful meeting is combining work with play.

Choose from many local attractions, outdoor activities, and the thrills of hot casino action.

Traveler info:
Distance: Approx. 4 miles from Parkway
For more info:
Harrah's Cherokee Casino
777 Casino Dr.
Cherokee, NC 28719
(800) HARRAHS (427-7247)
(828) 497-7777
www.harrahs.com

The spacious ballroom is available for conferences and events.

6 B *Please refer to map*

NC TOURISM

The Joyce Kilmer Wilderness Area is 3,800 acres of old-growth forest and is home to hemlock, sycamore, dogwood, beech and several species of oak.

are available via the incline railway. The dam forms Fontana Lake, which stretches 29 miles and offers water sports and fishing. Nearby **Historic Fontana Village** offers accommodations, restaurants and recreation in a village setting.

Joyce Kilmer Memorial Forest ⑪

Cheoah Ranger District
Route 1, Box 16-A,
Robbinsville, NC 28771
(828) 479-6431
www.main.nc.us/graham/
hiking/joycekil.html
•From MP 469 take U.S.
74/U.S. 19 to N.C. 143 west
into Graham County
•One of the few remaining
virgin hardwood tracts in the
Appalachians

Named for the poet/journalist who wrote "Trees," **Joyce Kilmer Memorial Forest** is home to 400-year-old poplars that are more than 20 feet in cir-

Fontana Dam/ Lake ⑩

Graham County N.C. Travel
and Tourism Authority
PO Box 575
North Main Street
Robbinsville, NC 28771
(828) 479-3790
(800) 470-3790
info@GrahamCountyTravel.com

www.grahamcountytravel.com
•MP 455.7, take U.S. 19

•The highest hydroelectric dam in the Eastern U.S.

Located in the Great Smoky Mountains, the Appalachian Trail actually crosses Fontana Dam, located in Graham County. Tours of the dam

---

The Cherokee Indian Reservation

...The Eastern Band of Cherokee Indians

Nestled in the heart of the Great Smoky Mountains is the homeland of the Cherokee Indians, the Cherokee Indian Reservation. The Qualla Boundary is a place of great history and culture.

Visit the beautiful land and waters of the Cherokee, a noble people with a love of

Call for your free visitor's guide.

Experience centuries of history and the culture of the Cherokee people.

the gifts of nature. Let us share with you the arts and crafts that have sustained us for centuries. See how we survived and what our life was like hundreds of years ago in our Indian village. Watch in amazement as the story of the tragic "Trail of Tears" unfolds in an outdoor drama. Visit our museum, or the surrounding area to enjoy internationally renowned trout fishing

waters, plus hiking, rafting and camping. All part of a great vacation in Cherokee.

Traveler info:
Exit: MP 469
Open: Year-round
For more info:
The Cherokee Indian
Reservation
PO Box 460
Cherokee, NC 28719
(800) 438-1601
www.cherokee-nc.com

VICKIE ROZEMA

The John C. Campbell Folk school has taught mountain crafts of all kinds for more than 70 years.

cumference and stand more than 100 feet high. A two-mile, figure-eight loop nature trail passes under the enormous trees in this 3,800-acre forest. The ground is covered with wildflowers, ferns and moss-covered logs from fallen giant trees. Located 15 miles from Robbinsville on N.C. 143 via U.S. 129.

John C. Campbell Folk School ⑫

One Folk School Road
Brasstown, NC 28902
(800)FOLK SCH
(828) 837-2775
Fax: (828) 837-8637
www.folkschool.org
•MP 443.1, take U.S. 74 to U.S. 64
•Founded in 1925 to preserve mountain crafts

Appalachian crafts are taught, exhibited and sold at **John C. Campbell Folk School**. Year-round instruction in traditional and contemporary crafts, folk music and nature studies are taught non-competitively; no grades or credits are given. The school, nestled on 380 acres, is housed in buildings on the National Register of Historic Places. The school's craft shop features juried work of more than 300 artists.

CATALOOCHEE RANCH®

Distance: Approx 4 miles from Parkway • 119 Ranch Dr. • Maggie Valley, NC 28751 • (800) 868-1401 • (828) 926-1401 • E-mail: info@cataloochee-ranch.com • Rates vary by unit • AE, MC, V

5,000 feet high, 1000 acres wide. Enjoy the wide open spaces on a mountain for all seasons. Luxurious rustic lodging, antiques, fireplaces, friendly horses, starry nights by the fire and much more, in the Great Smoky Mountains.

www.cataloocheeranch.com

NANTAHALA CABINS

Distance: Approx. 30 miles from Parkway • 580 Nantahala Cabins Ln. • Bryson City, NC 28713 • (877) 488-1622 • (828) 488-1622 • 8 cabins • $100-$225/night • Open: year-round • DC, MC, V • ঌ

Cabins have A/C and heat and are fully equipped; linen and bath towels are included. Some have hot tubs and fireplaces. New luxury log cabins. We offer whitewater rafting, horseback riding, mountain biking, hiking, fishing, and boating. Vacation planning available.

www.nantahalacabins.com

www.fryemontinn.com

BRYSON CITY FRYEMONT INN

Distance: Approx. 25 miles from Parkway • 245 Fryemont St. • Bryson City, NC 28713 • (800) 845-4879 • (828) 488-2159 • 37 rooms, 8 suites, 1 cabin • Rates: vary by season • DC, MC, V

A mountain tradition in fine lodging and dining. Casual elegance, rustic beauty, enormous stone fireplaces, gleaming hardwood floors. Excellent dining, full service bar, country breakfast, historic main lodge, and swimming pool.

www.cherokeeramada.com

RAMADA LIMITED CHEROKEE, NC

MP 469.1 • U.S. Hwy. 19 N. • Cherokee, NC 28719 • (800) 849-5263 • (828) 497-4231 • 90 rooms • $49-$149 • AE, DC, MC, V, Diners Club, Amoco • ঌ

Ramada Gold Key Award Winner, AAA Approved, All rooms have micro/fridge, TV, coffee/tea makers, hairdryers, irons/boards, and AM/FM Clock radio. FREE breakfast, casino shuttle, Jacuzzi rooms available. Across from casino parking lot.

Tennessee Smokies

Parkway MP 469 and Points West
Townsend • Gatlinburg • Pigeon Forge • Sevierville • Knoxville • Oak Ridge • Big South Fork

The mountain playland of Gatlinburg/Sevierville/Pigeon Forge also serves as a gateway to Great Smoky Mountains National Park and all its wonders. Elsewhere in this region are the urban charms of Knoxville and atom bomb history in the "secret city" of Oak Ridge.

There's plenty to see and do in this region. The state's highest point, Clingmans Dome, is here, and is accessible with only a short walk. So is the town where the first atomic bomb was built, Oak Ridge, a thriving little metropolis that used to not show up on roadmaps. Enjoy big city lights in Knoxville, peaceful beauty in Townsend and family fun at Dollywood in Pigeon Forge. Visit Cades Cove, a pioneer settlement and sheltered area of the Great Smoky Mountains National Park followed by shopping for crafts at the Great Smoky Arts & Crafts Community.

To the west of the Smokies are Tennessee Valley Authority lakes and all the recreation that goes with them, plus many historic small towns.

Known as the wedding capital of the South, Gatlinburg offers romantic hideaways in a mountain setting.

◁ *Deer are abundant in the Tennessee Smokies.*

Abrams Falls, accessed via a 2.5-mile hike from the Cades Cove Loop Trail, is one of the most popular spots in the Tennessee Smokies.

•The town of Dandridge has been touched by two first ladies. The only town in the country known to be named after Martha Dandridge Washington (George's wife), it was saved by a local woman's pleas to Eleanor Roosevelt, who convinced her husband to order a dike built to protect Dandridge from being flooded by the soon-to-be-built TVA Douglas Dam.

Getting Around

Parkway MP 461.9 marks the junction with U.S. 441, which winds its way around Gatlinburg and Pigeon Forge. An auto tour of Great Smoky Mountains National Park offers panoramic views, tumbling mountain streams, weathered historic buildings and miles of pristine forest.

Other favorite routes include Newfound Gap Road, which ascends about 3,000 feet up the spine of the Great Smoky Mountains, and the 7-mile Clingmans Dome Road, which follows a high ridge to the park's highest peak. Most of Middle East Tennessee's larger cities can be reached via I-40 or I-75.

KEY

- ▬ Highways
- — Secondary Roads
- ▬ Rivers/Lakes
- 🌳 State Park

•Seven miles east of Sevierville stands the Harrisburg Covered Bridge, constructed in 1875. Still used, it is 64 feet long in one span.

•Knoxville's Ijams Nature Center facility recruited some unusual employees to control their kudzu problem – a herd of goats.

Part of Mt. LeConte's magic is that it is acccess only on foot.

Buffalo Bill Fired Six-Shooters At Sullivan's

Patrick Sullivan's three-story, red-brick saloon was already known as "the" gathering spot for pioneers, hoodlums and gunslingers in Knoxville's then-unsavory railroad district when, on an October night in 1897, a brawl broke out in the bar and Buffalo Bill Cody fired his six-shooters into the ceiling. Today the restored Victoria pub serves up Irish-American fare in the heart of "Old City," a small, bustling district of restaurants, boutiques and galleries in turn-of-the-century warehouses.

N

Cumberland Gap
National Historical Park

Harrogate●

Powell River

25E

33

Clinch River

rris Lake

Big Ridge
State Park

11W

Cherokee
Lake

Panther Creek
State Park

33

House
Mountain
te Natural Area

Holston River

Morristown

Jefferson City

11E

81

7025W Dandridge

25E

40

66

Douglas Lake

Newport

321

French Broad River

Sevierville

411

25 70

9 A

441

321

Cosby●

40

A-D

5 Pigeon Forge

A-C

Townsend

4 Gatlinburg

7 6

441 Newfound
Gap Road

8

Great Smoky Mountains
National Park

1

10 miles

Cherokee Orchards Road in the Smokies is especially pretty at first snowfall.

JERRY WHALEY

SIGHTS AND SITES AT A GLANCE

1 Great Smoky Mountains
National Park
2 Cherohala Skyway
3 Lost Sea
4 Gatlinburg
  4 A Great Smoky
    Arts & Crafts
    Community
  4 B Chalet Village
    Properties
  4 C The Lodge at
    Buckberry Creek
  4 D Oak Square

4 E Reagan Properties
4 F Ripley's Aquarium of
  the Smokies
5 Pigeon Forge/Dollywood
  5 A Best Western Plaza
    Inn
  5 B Christmas Place at
    Bell Tower Square
  5 C Old Mill
  5 D ResortQuest Smoky
    Mountains
6 Townsend
7 Tuckaleechee Caverns

8 Cades Cove
9 Sevierville
  9 A Cove Mountain Resorts
10 Knoxville
11 Norris
  11 A Museum of Appalachia
12 Oak Ridge
13 Big South Fork National
  River and Recreation
  Area
See also:
  Traveler Services p. 119
  Trip Planner Listing p.130

For specific locations of state parks see www.state.tn.us/environment/parks or call 1-888-TN-PARKS.

Clingman's Dome, near the Tennessee/North Carolina border, is the highest peak in the Smokies, at 6,642 feet.

VICKIE ROZEMA

Great Smoky Mountains National Park ❶

National Park Headquarters
107 Park Headquarters Road
Gatlinburg, TN
(865) 436-1200
GRSM_Smokies_Information@
nps.gov
www.nps.gov/grsm
•MP 469
•More than a half-million acres
straddling the Tennessee/North
Carolina state line

Almost equally distributed between two states, the Great Smoky Mountains National Park is one of the largest protected areas east of the Rockies and home of one of the largest deciduous forests in the eastern U.S. Gatlinburg and Townsend are the gateways to the park from the Tennessee side and the Appalachian Trail runs the length of the park along the states' border.

The Tennessee half includes Cades Cove, an example of 19th-century mountain life, and Clingmans Dome, highest point in the state at 6,643 feet. Recreational opportunities abound here as do the multitudes of species that call the park home.

A trip to the Smokies is a wildlife-watcher's dream. Two hundred bird species, including red-eyed vireos, peregrine falcons and more than 30 kinds of warblers, can be spotted here. The Smokies serve as a refuge for 30 species of salamanders, a distinction that makes this the "salamander capital" of the United States. This is also home to the black bear (please look, but don't feed) and plenty of white-tailed deer, especially near Cades Cove, the oldest settlement in the area and an isolated preserve of pioneer life.

The park offers 1,008 developed sites in 10 campgrounds, plus 100 primitive back-country campsites on mountain ridges. Clingmans Dome is the highest point in the state. On clear days the view stretches for more than 100 miles. In spring and summer, a trek along the paved road from New-found Gap to the dome's summit allows up-close encounters with wildflowers.

If hiking isn't your

cup of tea, there are lots of other activities unfolding in Great Smoky Mountains National Park. Ask about annual festivals, bicycling, camping, fishing, educational programs, horseback riding, cross-country skiing, mountain life demonstrations, and free ranger-led walks and lectures. For more information see Great Smoky Mountain National Park on page 102.

The rose-breasted grosbeak is found in hardwood forests in late spring and summer.

ROB AND ANN SIMPSON

Cherohala Skyway ❷

Tellico Plains, TN to
Robbinsville, NC
(800) 245-5428
www.monroecounty.com
•Tenn. 165 off Tenn. 68
•A National Scenic Byway

As the Smoky Mountains straddle the state line, so does Cherohala Skyway. The road is a scenic east-west route connecting Tennessee and North Carolina. Travelers on the Tennessee side have breathtaking views of the Cherokee National Forest, including Bald River Falls. Kayaking and flyfishing are popular on the Tellico River, along the Skyway route. See page 103 for more information.

Lost Sea ❸

140 Lost Sea Rd.
Sweetwater, TN 37874
(423) 337-6616
www.thelostsea.com
•Off I-75 between Knoxville and Chatanooga
•Inside the cave, the temperature remains a constant 58 degrees

Listed by The Guinness Book of World Records as America's largest underground lake, the Lost Sea has earned another national distinction because of its rare crystalline anthodites (commonly called "cave flowers"), which are found in only a few caves around the world. The U.S. Department of the Interior designated the Lost Sea as a Registered Natural Landmark, an honor the site shares with such unique geological regions as the Cape Hatteras National Seashore and Yosemite National Park.

The caverns are known to have been used since the days of the Cherokees, but it wasn't until 1905 that a 13-year-old boy named Ben Sands wiggled through the tiny, muddy opening 300 feet underground and found himself in a huge room half filled with water. Today a one-hour tour of this popular Sweetwater attraction features a ride in a glass-bot-

Chalet Village Properties, Inc.

The Perfect Vacation Getaway

Only the amenities can compete with the scenery.

Book with confidence, established and family owned since 1972. 140 cabins and chalets, all fully furnished with fireplaces - many with hot tubs, views, pool tables and saunas. Our accommodations are affordable, comfortable and well appointed.

Gatlinburg and the surrounding area make it possible to enjoy a mountain vacation year-round with four seasons of activities. We are located within minutes of the national park, Ripley's Aquarium, ski lodge, Dollywood and outlet shopping. Call for our Springfest Special: stay three nights for the price of two from April to May 11, 2005.

Traveler info:
Distance: 33 Miles from Parkway
Open: 8:30-8:30 Mon.-Sat.
Rates: $90-$700
For more info:
Chalet Village Properties, Inc.
1441 Wiley Oakley Dr.
Gatlinburg, TN 37738
(800) 722-9617
www.chaletvillage.com

❹ **B** *Please refer to map*

Great Smoky Arts & Crafts Community

Drive the Historic Eight-Mile Loop

Look for the member logo, your assurance of authenicity.

The Great Smoky Arts & Crafts community is comprised of the largest group of independent artists and craftsmen in the country. This historic eight-mile loop of shops, studios and galleries has been designated a Tennessee Heritage Arts & Crafts trail and an official project of Save America's Treasures.

Make plans today to visit the Great Smoky Arts & Crafts Community where today's purchase is tomorrow's heirloom. All major credit cards are accepted and there's plenty of free parking.

Traveler info:
Distance: 33 Miles from Pkwy
Open: Daily
For more info:
Great Smoky Arts & Crafts Community
P.O. Box 807
Gatlinburg, TN 37738
(800) 565-7330
gsacc@msn.com
www.artsandcraftscommunity.com

❹ A *Please refer to map*

tomed boat and a 30-minute hike through the different rooms of the cave.

Gatlinburg ❹

Gatlinburg Chamber of Commerce
811 East Parkway
PO Box 527
Gatlinburg, Tennessee 37738
(800) 900-4148
Fax: (865) 430-3876
info@gatlinburg.com
www.gatlinburg.com
•MP 469, take US 441
•Wedding Capital of the South

Popular for weddings and honeymoons, Gatlinburg is also fun for the whole family. Ride the trolley to visit unique shops and galleries, then take the aerial tramway or skylift for spectacular mountain views. Accommodations here range from family motels to upscale resorts. Each season brings special events such as Smoky Mountain Music Festival, Harvest Festival and Winterfest Celebration.

Great Smoky Arts & Crafts Community ❹A

U.S. 321N/Glades Road/Buckhorn Road
P.O. Box 807
Gatlinburg,TN 37738
(800) 565-7330
(800) 900-4148
info@artsandcraftscommunity.com
www.artsandcraftscommunity.com
•MP 469, take U.S. 441
•The largest community of independent artisans in North America

This historic 8-mile loop has been designated a Tennessee Heritage Arts & Crafts Trail. Established in 1937, the artisans in this community paint, whittle, sew, carve and weave original works of art such as baskets, quilts, pottery, dolls, stained glass and watercolors in 80 shops and galleries. The area also features cafes and lodging. Take the orange Gatlinburg trolley if you don't want to drive. See page 111 for more information.

Gatlinburg, on U.S. 321 in Sevier County, offers a stunning array of shopping at the foot of the Smokies.

Ripley's Aquarium of the Smokies ❹F

88 River Road
Gatlinburg, TN 37738
(888) 240-1358
Fax: (865) 430-8818
www.ripleysaquariumofthesmokies.com
aquariumofthesmokies@ripleys.com
•MP 469, take U.S. 441
•Under the sea in the Smokies

See a tropical rain forest, coral reef or shark lagoon complete with 10-foot sharks in the Great Smoky Mountains, believe it or not. Ripley's Aquarium allows visitors to touch a stingray or walk through an underwater acrylic tunnel and see sand tigers and sharks just inches away. Open year-round, there are two restaurants on-site.

Live performers are part of the charm of Dollywood.

Pigeon Forge/ Dollywood ❺

Pigeon Forge Department of Tourism
PO Box 1390-I
Pigeon Forge, TN 37868
(800) 251-9100
(865) 453-8574
inquire@mypigeonforge.com
www.mypigeonforge.com
•MP 469, take US 441
•Fun in the mountains

Flanked by the Great Smoky Mountains, Pigeon Forge is home to outlet malls, gift shops and museums. More than 10 million visitors come here each year, most for **Dollywood**, a family theme park with shows, rides and year-round events.

Hailed by *The Wall Street Journal* as "the most popular attraction in Tennessee," the park features gospel, country and 1950s acts, craft demonstrations and plenty of down-home Southern cooking. At least 40 live performances unfold every day. The park also includes white-knuckle rides for the thrill-seekers, and Splash Country, a new water park, with waterfalls, wading pools and wild river rides (865) 428-9488.

And there's more to Pigeon Forge besides Dolly-

Arts and crafts shop abound around Gatlinburg offering crafts of the mountain past.

VICKIE ROZEMA

wood – visit the **Old Mill**, a restored 1830 mill now a restaurant overlooking the Little Pigeon River, next door to shops and galleries. Country music concerts and festivals (celebrating everything from quilts to the Wild West) fill Pigeon Forge's calendar, and there's shopping from outlets to Pigeon Forge's **Christmas Place** and fun family entertainment as well. Accommodations include hotels, cabins and resorts such as **Cove Mountain**. For more information see box on pages 115.

Townsend ⑥

Smoky Mountain Convention and Visitors Bureau
7906 E. Lamar Alexander Parkway
Townsend, TN 37882
(800) 525-6834
(865) 448-6134
www.smokymountains.org
•MP 469
•The Quiet Side of the Smokies

Foothills Parkway, called the Gateway to the Great Smoky Mountains, offers view after view of the park's majesty, climbing 18 miles up Chilhowee Mountain. Visit dozens of mountain craft and arts shops in the Townsend Art Community by following the Appalachian Arts & Crafts Directory, (800) 525-6834 or pick up a copy at the visi-

The Lodge at Buckberry Creek

Relax. Reminisce. Recapture.

Gatlinburg's first all-suite, luxury destination, The Lodge at Buckberry Creek combines the rustic elegance of Adirondack lodges with the pristine beauty of the Smoky Mountains of East Tennessee.

With 46 luxurious suites, this full-service resort has the warmth of a bed and breakfast, yet offers the refinement and expansive service of the great camps of the Adirondacks. Perfect for a romantic weekend or corporate powwow, Buckberry lets you experience nature without having to rough it - unless you want to.

④ c *Please refer to map*

Luxury in its natural habitat.

Traveler info:
Distance: 33 Miles from Parkway
Open: Daily; 24 hours
Rates: $175-$420
For more info:
The Lodge at Buckberry Creek
961 Campbell Lead Road
Gatlinburg, TN 37738
(866) 30-LODGE
www.buckberrylodge.com

Scenic View Rentals

Two Great Locations!

Our beautiful private chalets, condos and the new Comfort Inn Mountain River Suites offer the finest mountain accommodations. We provide you with all the comfort and conveniences of home, plus spectacular views of the Great Smoky Mountains. A large variety of units are available. Best of all, our competitive rates, special discounts and personalized service make Scenic View Rentals your unsurpassed Smoky Mountain getaway.

Oak Square - one of our many properties.

from Parkway
Open: Daily
Rooms: 100+
For more info:
Scenic View Rentals
685 River Rd.
Gatlinburg, TN 37738
(800) 423-5182
www.scenicviewrentals.com
www.oaksquare.net

Traveler info:
Distance: Approx. 8 miles
④ D *Please refer to map*

tors center. The **Townsend Heritage Festival and Old Timers' Day** offers traditional bluegrass music and Appalachian crafts amid the brilliant autumn hues and mountain scenery of the Great Smoky Mountains and Townsend. The two-day festival, held the last weekend in September, celebrates Appalachian culture, including music, storytelling, arts and crafts demonstrations, and the natural beauty of the Smoky Mountains.

Tuckaleechee Caverns ❼

825 Cavern Rd.
Townsend, TN
(865) 448-2274
info@tuckaleecheecaverns.com
www.tuckaleecheecaverns.com
•The gift shop and tour origin area built over the entrance are cooled by 58° air from the caverns.

As a 4-year-old boy growing up in the Dry Valley area of Townsend, the late Bill Vananda played in and around the same cave system that Native Americans had discovered and explored more than a century before. Tuckaleechee Caverns now draws nearly 100,000 visitors each year to see its illuminated rock and crystal formations.

Vananda's sons, Phillip and Steven, along with their families, operate the busi-

PAT & CHUCK BLACKLEY

Bud Ogle built this cabin, now in the Great Smokies National Park, for his family in 1879 and used many innovative techniques in construction, including running water in the form of a log flume that poured directly into a sink inside.

ness their father started with partner Harry Myers in 1953.

From March 15 through November 15, visitors tour the mile-long path through the caverns to see the stalagmites, stalactites, stream passage and other formations that are as old as the surrounding mountains. They enter the cool, damp quiet of the cave, just off U.S. 321, and listen to the calcite dripping from the stalactites.

Cades Cove ❽

Near Townsend, off U.S. 321
(865) 436-1227
GRSM_Smokies_Information@
nps.gov
www.cadescoveopp.com
•MP 469

•An open-air museum of pioneer life

Millions of visitors seek out this unique spot nestled in the Great Smoky Mountains each year. Cades Cove preserves history, pioneer culture, natural beauty, wildlife and endangered plants. Visit the operational grist mill with working waterwheel plus late 19th- and 20th-century churches and cabins. Try the 11-mile, one-way loop road to see the sights; hiking and biking are also popular.

You're likely to spot a group of "settlers" making sorghum molasses, lye soap and apple butter; wild turkeys and deer silhouetted by rustic barns, churches and cabins; and a water-powered gristmill that once served the entire community. This is one of the most popular spots in the Smokies for hiking and biking.

Along the trail, more than 70 historic buildings beckon travelers to stop, park and explore. (It's a good idea to buy a $1 tour booklet.) Built in the 1820s, the **John Oliver Cabin** is the oldest log home in Cades Cove; the cabin's notched corners are held together by gravity instead

WILLIE JOHNSON

The Cades Cove Loop Road in Great Smoky Mountains National Park is open to cyclists on Saturdays and Wednesdays, May to September.

Pigeon Forge, Tennessee

Experience the Fun and Excitement of a Family Get-away to Action-packed Pigeon Forge.

Pigeon Forge is the adventure your family's been waiting for. Tucked in the Tennessee foothills next to Great Smoky Mountains National Park, Pigeon Forge is the capital of family fun. From Parkway rides to Dollywood to dazzling live shows, the excitement is all within city limits. Add in a good helping of restaurants, outlet and specialty shopping and more than 8,500 hotel rooms, and you've got the perfect family getaway!

Along the Pigeon Forge Parkway, there are more than 50 fun-filled attractions. Race around the go-cart track or have a splash in the bumper boats. Challenge your friends and family to a round or two of miniature golf or try out the thrilling indoor skydiving simulator!

Pigeon Forge is home to a variety of theaters featuring all styles of music - Broadway, rock n' roll, country, bluegrass, gospel

Pigeon Forge is located five miles north of the entrance to Great Smoky Mountains National Park.

and more. Hilarious comedy and amazing feats of magic complete the entertainment lineup.

A Smoky Mountain family adventure awaits kids of all ages at Dollywood, now celebrating its 20th anniversary. Enjoy incredible festivals plus spectacular shows, master craftsmen and thrilling rides, including an expanded Country Fair Area featuring ten new family rides.

For more information on all the great things there are to see and do in Pigeon Forge, call 1-800-753-6543 or visit us online.

Talented riders perform tricks and stunts on horseback at Dolly Parton's Dixie Stampede.

Traveler info:
Distance: 20 miles from Parkway
For more info:
Pigeon Forge Department of Tourism
PO Box 1390
Pigeon Forge, TN 37203
(800) 753-6543
www.mypigeonforge.com

Feel the thrill of The Thunderhead™, a state-of-the-art wooden roller coaster at Dollywood.

5 *Please refer to map*

Davy Crockett is one focus of Knoxville's East Tennessee Historical Society Museum.

COURTESY STATE OF TENNESSEE

www.seviervillechamber.org
•MP 469, take US 441
•Dolly Parton's Hometown

Stop by Sevierville's courthouse to see a statue of the town's native daughter. Then shop till you drop at the antique and outlet malls such as **Governor's Crossing Outlet Center**, 212 Collier Dr. or **Tanger Five Oaks Outlet Center**, 1645 Parkway Ste. 960, (865) 453-1053. Watch a **Tennessee Smokies** (AA affiliate, St. Louis Cardinals) baseball game at nearby Kodak, off I-40 (888) 978-2288.

of nails or pegs. **The Methodist Church**, built by J.D. McCampbell for $115, was organized in the 1820s. The cove has become a haven for many types of wildlife. Red wolves were introduced a decade ago in an effort to find an environment where these endangered animals could survive. Bears and European wild boars can often be seen at the pull-off points.

Sevierville   ⑨

Sevierville Chamber of Commerce
And Convention & Visitors Bureau
110 Gary Wade Blvd.
Sevierville, TN 37862
(888) SEVIERVILLE
(888) SMOKY-4U x 44
(865) 453-6411
info@seviervillechamber.com

Knoxville   ⑩

Knoxville Convention and Visitors Bureau
601 W. Summit Hill Dr., #200B
Knoxville, TN 37902
(800) 727-8045
(865) 523-7263
tourism@knoxville.org
www.knoxville.org
•From terminus of Parkway at 469, take U.S. 40 to Knoxville
•The Tennessee Smokies' "Big City"

Visit Knoxville, home of the University of Tennessee, for a myriad of restaurants, shopping, museums and family fun. **Knoxville Zoo** has the largest variety of indigenous and non-indigenous animals housed in natural habitats in the area. 3500 Knoxville Zoo Drive, Exit 392 off I-40. (865) 637-5331. Visit the Old City Historic District or try a dinner cruise on the **Star of Knoxville** sternwheeler on the Tennessee River (865) 525-STAR.

Museum of Appalachia   ⑪ A

Highway 61
P.O. Box 1189
Norris, TN 37828
(865) 494-7680 or 494-0514
www.museumofappalachia.com
museumappalachia@bellsouth.net
musofapp@icx.net
•From Parkway Terminus at 469 to U.S. 40 to Knoxville, U.S.75 north to Norris
•Preserving the Appalachian way of life

Pigeon Forge Best Westerns

Plaza Inn and Toni Inn

Same excellent service and accommodations, two great locations! Let Best Western Plaza Inn or Best Western Toni Inn be your choice for group meetings, reunions and family vacations when planning your trip to Pigeon Forge, TN along the Blue Ridge Parkway. With great locations just minutes from an array of dining, recreation and attraction choices, we offer a variety of amenities sure to please all travelers.

Visible through your window may be a spectacular view of Smoky Mountain peaks!

For more info:
Best Western Toni Inn
3810 Parkway
Pigeon Forge, TN 37863
(800) 422-3232
www.bestwesterntoniinn.com

Best Western Plaza Inn
3755 Parkway
Pigeon Forge, TN 37863
(800) 232-5656
www.bestwesternplazainn.com

Traveler info:
Distance: Approx. 20 miles from Parkway

⑤ A *Please refer to map*

Called "the most authentic and complete replica of Pioneer Appalachian life," Founder/Director John Rice Irwin's Museum of Appalachia is a 65-acre farm/village with more than 30 log cabins and buildings, 250,000 artifacts plus farm animals, the Appalachian Hall of Fame and gardens. Events include Tennessee Fall Homecoming and July 4th Celebration and Anvil Shoot.

Mountain crafts are demonstrated at the Museum of Appalachia.

COURTESY STATE OF TENNESSEE

Norris   ⑪

Anderson County Tourism Council
115 Welcome Ln.
Clinton, TN 37716
(800) 524-3602
info@yallcome.org
www.yallcome.org
• From terminus of Parkway at MP 469, take U.S. 40 to Knoxville, U.S. 75 north to Norris.
• A classic TVA community

Under President Franklin Roosevelt's New Deal, Norris was built by TVA nearly 70 years ago while the dam with the same name was under construction to bring electricity to the more than 90 percent of the region which had none. The goal was to create a self-sustaining town, a showcase for rural electrification and cooperative industry. Norris was planned to be fully electric with all the modern conveniences. Surrounded

Christmas Place at Bell Tower Square

One of the Country's Largest and Most Beautiful Christmas Villages

Christmas Place has something new for everyone in 2005. Old world charm awaits you as you stroll around the picturesque courtyard with its lush gardens and outdoor railway. Then, enter a Christmas fantasyland with gifts and decorations from around the world. You will be awed by the beautiful displays and decorated trees. See Santa soar through the starry sky on his famous Christmas Eve ride! Everyone will enjoy our renovated fun, family-oriented toy & train

Bell Tower Square. It's Worth The Trip!

store. Call for our specialty catalog or visit us online.

Traveler info:
Distance: 26 miles from Parkway
For more info:
Christmas Place at Bell Tower Square
2470 Parkway
Pigeon Forge, TN 37863
(800) 445-3396
(865) 453-0415
www.christmasplace.com/br

⑤ **B** *Please refer to map*

ResortQuest Smoky Mountains

Smoky Mountain Memories ... Closer Than You Think

Nestled in the heart of the Great Smoky Mountains National Park, Pigeon Forge and Gatlinburg, Tennessee is one of the most beautiful and popular vacation destinations! With over 300,000 acres of National Forest, you'll enjoy hiking trails, white water rafting, fishing & horseback riding. Our GolfView Resort is the closest resort to Dollywood!

Discover all this nature lover's paradise has to offer while staying in one of ResortQuest's Mountain Cabins, Resort Cabins and Luxury Condos.

Wedding and honeymoon packages are available.

Traveler info:
Distance: Less than 5 miles from Parkway
For more info:
ResortQuest Smoky Mountains
718 GolfView Blvd.
Pigeon Forge, TN 37863
(888) 255-8343
smokyrentals@resortquest.com
www.resortquestsmokymountains.com

⑤ **D** *Please refer to map*

The Old Mill Square

A Unique Shopping Experience

The Old Mill Square's Pigeon River Pottery has been home to pottery making for over 40 years. In-house artisans form, fire and glaze each piece to create truly one-of-a-kind sculptures – from functional dinnerware to skillfully crafted art. The square's other shops include the Candy Kitchen, Farmhouse Kitchen, Toy Bin and Potting Shed. Traditional southern fare is offered at the Old Mill Restaurant, and artisan-style breads using the mill's stone-ground grains are baked fresh daily at the Old Mill Bakery Café.

Take a guided tour through our famous grist mill, which has been in operation since 1830.

Traveler info:
Distance: Approx. 40 miles from Parkway
Open: Daily
For more info:
The Old Mill Square
175 Old Mill Ave.
Pigeon Forge, TN 37863
(865) 453-1104
www.old-mill.com

5 **c** *Please refer to map*

Cove Mountain Resort Located in Wears Valley

The Gateway to the Smokies

Located in beautiful Wears Valley, between Pigeon Forge and Townsend, and bordered by the Great Smoky Mountains National Park. We offer a variety of luxuriously rustic log cabins, chalets and cottages, ranging from one to six bedrooms. Come and enjoy our fantastic views, swimming pools, hot tubs, whirlpool spas, fireplaces, and covered porches with rockers. We specialize in beautiful mountain views and much more. Our greatest attraction is your complete satisfaction.

Enjoy beautiful views from our rental cabins and chalets.

Traveler info:
Distance: Approx. 48 miles from Parkway
Open: Daily; 8am-10pm
Rates: $65-$450
For more info:
Cove Mountain Resorts
3202 Wears Valley Rd.
Sevierville, TN 37862
(800) 559-5325
(865) 429-5577
www.covemountain.com

9 **A** *Please refer to map*

by a forest buffer, the town had one of the first greenbelts, with numerous footpaths.

The planned utopia operated like a company town; TVA operated almost everything from the gas station to the town's cafeteria. But there were also dreams of a self-sustaining community. One of President Roosevelt's challenges was to help the people of the valley make the most of their natural resources. When white clay or kaolin – necessary for fine porcelain – was discovered near Spruce Pine, N.C., a lab at Norris was equipped to turn the clay into fine porcelain.

But the lab was closed by 1938. The two-story ceramics lab still stands today, used by TVA's engineering department.

When the dam was completed, the workers left Norris and professionals who worked in Knoxville or Oak Ridge moved in. The federal government sold the town in 1948 to a private corporation that then sold lots to individuals.

Today, Norris School, once the largest electrically heated building in the world, serves as a middle school. The cafeteria where TVA workers in the 1930s ate a full meal for 25 cents still stands. The old workers' dormitory is now used for Methodist Sunday school classes. As with most utopias, Norris had its flaws. But it has grown to become a nice place to live and visit.

For more information: The New Deal Network (newdeal.feri.org/tva) and TVA's website (www.tva.gov/heritage).

Oak Ridge **12** "The Secret City"

Oak Ridge Convention and Visitors Bureau
302 South Tulane Avenue
Oak Ridge, TN 37830-6726
(800) 887-3429

Big South Fork River and Recreation Area provide some of the best outdoor recreation in the Southeast.

(865) 482-7821
info@oakridgevisitor.com
www.oakridgevisitor.com
•From terminus of Parkway at 469, take U.S. 40 to Knoxville, then Tenn. 62 to Tenn. 162
•World War II's Secret City built in 1942

Not many would have guessed that the first

atomic bomb would be built in East Tennessee, as part of the Manhattan Project, in a picturesque town built to order by the Government during World War II. Today, visitors can see the project's Graphite Reactor or take a **Secret City Scenic Excursion Train tour**. Oak Ridge is also home to the **American Museum of Science & Energy**.

Big South Fork National River and Recreation Area  ⑬

4564 Leatherwood Rd.
Oneida, TN 37841
(423) 286-7275
BISO_Information@nps.gov
www.nps.gov/biso
•From Parkway terminus at 469 to U.S. 40 to Knoxville, U.S. 75 north to Tenn. 63 and 297 into Scott County

•Big recreational fun

Named for the Big South Fork of the Cumberland River which passes through 90 miles of gorges and valleys within its boundaries, this national park has more than 110,000 acres of wild area bordering the Kentucky state line. Recreational opportunities abound with camping, whitewater rafting, hiking plus horseback riding on more than 200 miles of trails. Natural beauty is abundant here. There's Cumberland Falls, considered the most impressive eastern waterfall next to Niagara Falls, and Colditz Cove Natural Area, where curiosity-seekers can venture behind a 60-foot waterfall. Also, don't miss the wildflower walks at Frozen Head State Park and the awe-inspiring natural arches

TENNESSEE SMOKIES SERVICES

CANEY CREEK CABINS

Distance: Approx. 38 miles from Parkway • 792 Caney Creek Rd. • Pigeon Forge, TN 37863 • (800) 273-5116 • (865) 436-9091 • E-mail: info@caneycreek.com • Open: Mon.-Sat. 8am-10pm, Sun. 1pm-5pm

Our cozy secluded vacation cabins offer one of the best values for family vacations in the Smoky Mountains. Enjoy Bass and Trout fishing in our private lake. Conveniently located between Pigeon Forge and Gatlinburg.

www.caneycreek.com

www.forbiddencavern.com

FORBIDDEN CAVERNS

Distance: Approx. 50 miles from Parkway • 455 Blowing Cave Rd. • Sevierville, TN 37876 • (865) 453-5972 • Open: Daily Apr.-Oct. • Admission: Adults $10; Children 5-12 $5; under 4 Free

An educational tour of sparkling formations, towering chimneys, grottos and a crystal clear stream. Special lighting effects and stereophonic sound presentation combine to make your visit truly enjoyable.

GATLINBURG REAL ESTATE & RENTALS

Distance: Approx. 33 miles from Parkway • 211 Parkway • Gatlinburg, TN 37738 • (800) 359-1661 • Open: Daily 9am-9pm • Rates: $85-$550/day • AE, DC • &

Experience the elegance of the south. We have the finest accommodations in the Smokies. Enjoy a cozy romantic night in front of the fire, or sit in the hot tub and gaze at the breathtaking views of the Smoky Mountains. An unforgetable experience awaits our guests.

www.gatlinburgchalets.com

TENNESSEE SMOKIES SERVICES

LOST SEA

Distance: Approx. 70 miles from Parkway • 140 Lost Sea Rd. • Sweetwater, TN 37874 • (423) 337-6616 • • Hours: vary depending on season • MC, V

Discover the lost sea, America's largest underground lake and Registered Natural Landmark. Cavern tours include a glass bottom boat ride across the incredible lake. Other facilities include the Cavern Kitchen, and General Store.

www.thelostsea.com

MOUNTAIN LAUREL CHALETS

Distance: Approx. 33 miles from Parkway • 440 Ski Mountain Rd. • Gatlinburg, TN 37738 • (800) 784-6532 • (865) 436-5277 • Open: Daily 8am-9pm • 150 rooms • Rates: $95-$1,000/day • AE, MC, V • ♿

Offering quality chalets for 30 years, choose from 150 chalets from 1-12 bedrooms in the mountains above Gatlinburg. Hot tubs, pool table, sweeping mountain views or secluded woods. Book online at www.mtnlaurelretreats.com.

RAMADA INN AND CONVENTION CENTER

Distance: Approx. 30 miles from Parkway • 4010 Parkway. • Pigeon Forge, TN 37863 • (800) 523-3919 • Rooms: 122 rooms and suites • AE, DC, MC, V, D • ♿

Ramada Inn is located on the Parkway near all area attractions and is next to The Smoky Mountain Convention Center, a 20,000 sq. ft. facility ready for your next meeting or convention.

www.smokymountainresorts.com

RAMADA INN FOUR SEASONS

Distance: Approx. 30 miles from Parkway • 756 Parkway. • Gatlinburg, TN 37738 • (800) 933-8678 • (865) 436-7881 • Open: 24 hrs. • AE, V, MC, D

The beauty, service, spacious facilities and location of the Ramada Inn Four Seasons have made it a favorite for vacationers and business travelers for generations. Located in the center of Gatlinburg we offer all the amenities including an indoor heated pool.

www.reaganresorts.com

RAMADA INN

Distance: Approx. 130 miles from Parkway • US 25E Hwy. 58 • Cumberland Gap, TN 37724 • (423) 869-3637 • 150 rooms • AE, DC, MC, V, • ♿

Historic Cumberland Gap, TN is located at the junction where TN, KY and VA meet. Experience historical tourism at its best: Appalachian arts & crafts, civil war and colonial re-enactments, outdoor recreation, Cumberland Gap National Historical Park and more.

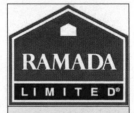

RAMADA LIMITED EAST KNOXVILLE

Distance: Approx. 10 miles from Parkway • 722 Brakebill Rd. • Knoxville, TN 37924 • (865) 546-7271 • Rates: $60-$110 • Rooms: 58 • AE, V, MC, DC • ♿

Ramada Limited - East is located between the Great Smoky Mountains and downtown Knoxville. Complimentary executive breakfast served daily, high speed Internet, microwave and refrigerator, plus a coffee maker, hairdryer, digital safe and outdoor pool.

www.theramada.com/knoxville02543

TENNESSEE SMOKIES SERVICES

SMOKY MOUNTAINS TOWNSEND, TN

Distance: Approx. 45 minutes from Parkway • 7906 E. Lamar Alexander Parkway • Townsend, TN 37882 • (800) 525-6834

Enjoy the mountain air of Townsend, Tennessee - the peaceful side of the Smokies. Stay in a cabin, hotel, bed & breakfast, or at a campsite. Enjoy arts/crafts, hiking, biking, tubing, and horseback riding. Call 800-525-6834 or visit our website for a free vacation guide.

www.smokymountains.org

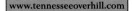

www.tennesseeoverhill.com

CHEROHALA SCENIC BYWAY - OCOEE SCENIC BYWAY

Distance: Approx. 55 miles from Parkway • P O Box 143 • Etowah, TN 37331 • (423) 263-7232 • E-mail: info@ tennesseeoverhill.com

Discover the Tennessee Overhill on two national scenic byways. Explore the regions unique attractions, heritage areas, museums, antique shops and the Cherokee National Forest while traveling the scenic highways and backroads in southeast Tennessee.

THE PARK GRILL RESTAURANT

Distance: Approx. 33 miles from Parkway • 1110 Parkway • Gatlinburg, TN 37738 • (865) 436-2300 • E-mail: caroline@peddlerparkgrill.com • Open: Mon.-Sun. 5pm • AE, DC, MC, V • & • Fax: 865-436-2836.

The Park Grill – Featuring fresh Smoky Mountain Trout. Free & huge salad bar included with all entrees. Moonshine Chicken. Rainbow Trout. BBQ Ribs. Homemade desserts. Full bar. Great children's menu. Same owners as The Peddler.

www.peddlerparkgrill.com

RAMADA LIMITED PIGEON FORGE, TN

Distance: Approx. 48 miles from Parkway • 2193 Parkway • Pigeon Forge, TN 37863 • (800) 269-1222 • Rates: $49-$160 • V, MC, AE, DC • &

We offer individual packages, a free continental breakfast, refrigerators/microwaves, hair dryers, ironing boards and coffee makers. Convenient to Dollywood, the Great Smoky Mountains, all major attractions, dining and 200 name brand outlets.

www.pigeonforgeramada.com/brptg1

www.smokymountainresorts.com

CLOSEST HOTEL TO DOLLYWOOD

Distance: Approx. 30 miles from Parkway • 239 Dollywood Ln. • Pigeon Forge, TN 37863 • (800) 523-3919 • E-mail: smr@icx.net • 53 suites • AE, MC, V, DC • &

Ramada Limited Suites offers the best in accommodations and location in Pigeon Forge with spacious rooms, pool, fitness center and more! We are just minutes away from a championship golf course and Dollywood.

RAMADA LIMITED EXIT 407 I-40

Distance: Approx. 50 miles from Parkway • 3385 Winfield Dunn Pkwy. • Kodak, TN 37764 • (800) 348-4652 • Open: 24 hrs. • Rooms: 80 • AE, V, MC, DC • &

Just off the Interstate, the gateway to action-filled Pigeon Forge, Gatlinburg, and the Great Smoky Mountains. 45 minutes to Knoxville and 20 minutes to Pigeon Forge; indoor pool, Whirlpool units, free breakfast, plus children stay free. Adjacent to restaurant.

www.ramadalimitedkodak.com

Northeast Tennessee

MP 469 and Points North and West
Bristol • Elizabethton • Erwin • Greeneville •
Johnson City • Jonesborough • Kingsport • Rogersville

History is palpable in this part of Tennessee, with the heritage of Davy Crockett and Daniel Boone still alive. More recently, country music had its birth in Bristol, and the great works of the Tennessee Valley Authority changed the look of the land.

Follow the path of the Old Stage Road through Northeast Tennessee and see the state's oldest town, oldest building, oldest frame house, first territorial capital and last covered bridge in use. Tour Rocky Mount, Tipton-Haynes farm or the Exchange Place to see Northeast Tennessee history come to life. Enjoy outdoor fun at parks like Warrior's Path near Kingsport, or go boating on one of the TVA-made lakes: South Holston, Boone or Watauga.

The little cities of the region are home not only to repositories of history, but also festivals and events throughout the year. Among the most noted is the Jonesborough Storytelling Festival. Take your time and enjoy this corner of Tennessee.

COURTESY EAST TENN. MARKETING PARTNERSHIP

Little shops line the street of downtown Jonesborough, Tenn., adding a festive atmosphere to the town.

◁ *Catawba Rhododendron provide the key colors each early summer near Roan Mountain.*

VICKIE ROZEMA

Roan Mountain State Resort Park offers great fall foliage.

Getting Around

Interstate 81 carries primary north-south traffic through the Northeast Tennessee region, connecting Bristol and Morristown and then continuing south to Knoxville. I-181 connects Kingsport and Johnson City, intersecting with 81 about halfway between the two cities. From Johnson City, the route continues south to Erwin. Jonesborough, south of Johnson City, is reached from there via U.S.11E/321. U.S. routes 421, 321 and 19E cross the region in a generally east-west direction, with 321 turning south and Johnson City toward Greeneville.

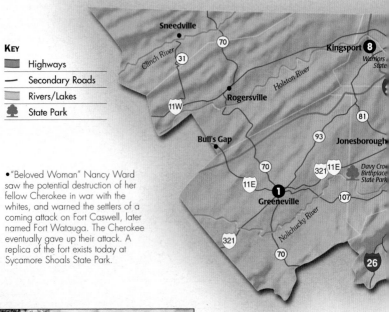

KEY

- Highways
- Secondary Roads
- Rivers/Lakes
- State Park

Sneedville

Clinch River · 31 · 70

Kingsport 8

Warriors State

Holston River

Rogersville

11W

Bull's Gap

81

93

Jonesborough

70

321 · 11E

Davy Crockett Birthplace State Park

11E

1 Greeneville

107

• "Beloved Woman" Nancy Ward saw the potential destruction of her fellow Cherokee in war with the whites, and warned the settlers of a coming attack on Fort Caswell, later named Fort Watauga. The Cherokee eventually gave up their attack. A replica of the fort exists today at Sycamore Shoals State Park.

Nolichucky River

321

70

26

DAVID REED

• Elvis played his last appearance as an opening act in Kingsport; paid $37 for a half hour of music, he went on to Memphis and became a legend.

The covered bridge at Elizabethton is the site of an annual covered bridge festival.

20 Million Rainbow Trout From Northeast Tennessee

Congress authorized a fish hatchery near Erwin in 1894, with operations beginning in 1897. In the early days, fish were distributed via railcars. By 1976, the hatchery had converted to a brood stock and egg operation, producing up to 20 million rainbow trout eggs a year for shipping to state, federal and foreign hatcheries.

• Roan Mountain has some of the largest grassy balds – treeless peaks – in the world. No one knows the reasons for these vast high spaces, though theories include early grazing animals, forest fires and the influence of humans.

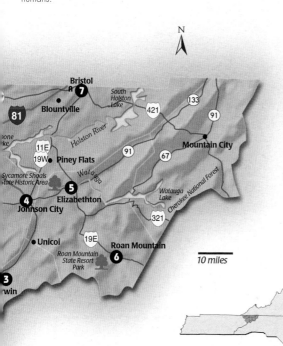

COURTESY NETTA

At Rocky Mount, costumed interpreters present life on the 18th-century frontier.

10 miles

• The high altitude and protected environment of Shady Valley enabled its cranberry plants to survive the last ice age (and, barely, the altering of a stream course by the U.S. Army Corps of Engineers). Every October the town celebrates with a Cranberry Festival.

• The first publications in the nation devoted entirely to the abolition of human slavery were published in Jonesborough.

SIGHTS AND SITES AT A GLANCE

❶ Greeneville Area
❷ Jonesborough Area
　❷ⓐ International Storytelling Center
❸ Erwin Area
❹ Johnson City
❺ Elizabethton Area
❻ Roan Mountain State Park

❼ Bristol Area
❽ Kingsport Area
　❽ⓐ Bays Mountain

See also:
Traveler Services p. 129
Trip Planner Listing p. 130

For specific locations of state parks see www.state.tn.us/environment/parks or call 1-888-TN-Parks

Greeneville Area ❶

Greene County Partnership
Tourism Council
115 Academy Street
Greeneville, TN 37743
(423) 638-4111
Fax: (423) 638-5345
gcp@xtn.net
www.greenecountypartnership.
com
•Visit Davy Crockett's birthplace

Visit the restored cabin marking the birthplace of the famous frontiersman at **Davy Crockett Birthplace State Park**. 1245 Davy Crockett Park Road, Limestone. (423) 257-2167.

Crockett and Andrew Jackson were guests at **Dickson-Williams Mansion** (1815). 108 N. Irish St., Greeneville. (423) 787-0500.

Tour the home of the first impeached president at **Andrew Johnson National Historic Site** including the Johnson House (1830s), museum and cemetery where Johnson is buried. 121 Monument Avenue, Greeneville. (423) 638-3551.

Jonesborough Area ❷

Historic Jonesborough Tourism
Cooperative
111 W. Main Street, Suite 202
Jonesborough, TN 37659
(423) 753-1011
(877) 913-1612
Fax: (423) 913-2642
info@historicjonesborough.com
www.historicjonesborough.com
•Tennessee's oldest town

Stroll the brick sidewalks of Tennessee's oldest town and enjoy shops and restaurants housed in historic buildings. **Jonesborough/Washington County History Museum** displays maps and artifacts dating back 200 years. 117 Boone Street (in the visitors' center), Jonesborough. (423) 753-1011. Spend the night at **Hawley House B&B**, the oldest structure in town, restored with antiques and folk art. 114 E. Woodrow Avenue, Jonesborough. (423) 753-8869.

Step back 225 years in history when walking through historic Jonesborough. Many buildings from the town's early days still stand, including the historic Chester Inn, built in 1797.

KINGSPORT CVB

International Storytelling Center ❷ Ⓐ

116 W. Main Street
Jonesborough, TN 37659
(800) 952-8392
(423) 753-2171
Fax: (423) 913-8219
info@storytellingcenter.net
www.storytellingcenter.net

After many years of hosting the National Storytelling Festival in Jonesborough, the **International Storytelling Center** was built in Tennessee's oldest

TENN. MEDIA SERVICES

Fly fishing is terrific in the rivers of Northeast Tennessee.

town. The only facility in the world dedicated to storytelling, the center provides education programs, displays and museum exhibits. The 200-year-old **Chester Inn**, original home of the center, is part of the complex.

Erwin Area ❸

Unicoi County Chamber of
Commerce
100 S. Main Ave.
P.O. Box 713,
Erwin, TN 37650-0713
(423) 743-3000
Fax: (423) 743-0942
info@unicoicounty.org
www.unicoicounty.org
•Try the Nolichucky's
whitewater

Blue Ridge Pottery, railroad history and turn-of-the-century Main Street shops are displayed at **Unicoi County Heritage Museum**. Located in a 1903 restored home on the grounds of **Erwin National Fish Hatchery**, 1715 Johnson City Highway, Erwin. (423) 743-4712 .

Enjoy whitewater on the **Nolichucky River** as it winds through the deepest gorge in the Eastern U.S. Hike or fish in the **Cherokee National Forest** (423) 476-9700.

Johnson City Area ❹

Johnson City Convention and
Visitors Bureau
603 E. Market St.,
P.O. Box 180
Johnson City, TN 37605-0180
(423) 461-8000
(800) 852-3392
Fax: (423) 461-8047
www.johnsoncitytnchamber.com
•Home of East Tennessee State
University

Home to ETSU, **John-son City** has plenty to see and do. For children, **Hands-On! Regional Museum** features interactive exhibits 315 E. Main St. (423) 434-HAND or visit **Tipton-Haynes Historic Site**, a restored 18th-century home, 2620 S. Roan St. (423) 926-3631.

See history live at **Rocky Mount**, 200 Hyder Hill, Piney Flats, (1770) oldest original territorial capital in the U.S. (423) 538-7396. For more information see box below.

KINGSPORT CVB

Even kids get involved in historic re-enactions in Rocky Mount, famous for its comprehensive costumed interpretive guides and performances.

Elizabethton Area ❺

Elizabethton/Carter County
Tourism Council
500 Veteran Memorial Pkwy.
PO Box 190
Elizabethton, TN 37644-0190
(423) 547-3852
Fax: (423) 547-3854
info@tourelizabethton.com
www.tourelizabethton.com

•See one of the oldest covered bridges in Tennessee

Sycamore Shoals State Historic Area marks the first permanent American settlement west of the original 13 colonies. The Overmountain Men mustered here before the battle of King's Mountain. Tour the museum and recon-

---

Johnson City, Tennessee

Discover Your Own Pioneer Spirit

Drop into this beautiful, engaging region and discover a world of historical treasures, bluegrass music and extraordinary outdoor experiences.

Described as "Where the Pioneer Spirit Began," Johnson City is home to Rocky Mount, a living history attraction still functioning as though it's the year 1791.

A long-time tradition

Adventure down the Nolichucky River.

❹ *Please refer to map*

of mountain music thrives in clubs and eateries and shows up in downtown street festivals, like the Blue Plum in June.

Neighboring Jonesborough—Tennessee's oldest town and home to the National Storytelling Festival—is highlighted by quaint inns and shops along a main street suited for stagecoaches.

Vibrant hospitality is positioned near an extraordinary landscape that includes the Appalachian Trail, fishing streams, Roan Mountain State Park, bike trails and the mighty Nolichucky River.

For information, go to visitjohnsoncitytn.com. Explore Northeast Tennessee and experience the online tour: "Tales and Trails of America's First Frontier" at netta.com.

Pick-up bands and mountain music show up in clubs, eateries and street festivals.

Traveler info:
Distance: 55 miles from Parkway
For more info:
Johnson City Convention and Visitor's Bureau
603 East Market St.
Johnson City, TN 37605
(800) 852-3392, Ext. BR
www.visitjohnsoncitytn.com

Racing Around

Racing has been a Southern Appalachian tradition since the early days of moonshining. Bootleggers would race their cars in and around the area to see whose vehicle was fastest; from that, the behemoth that is NASCAR was born. Because of its origins, it's only fitting that one of the biggest and the best NASCAR tracks is in the Blue Ridge Mountains, the Bristol Motor Speedway.

Get into racing excitement at one of NASCAR's biggest venues at the Bristol Motor Speedway.

The speedway one of the biggest sports venues in the country, with seats for 160,000 fans. There is an oval raceway where stock car and truck racing occurs, and the Bristol Dragway for drag racing.

Aside from huge racing events, there are driving schools to learn how to drive stock cars, and even drive around the oval, track tours, and their free Fan Zone, an interactive experience with a drag racing simulator, videogames, a movie on the history of the speedway, and one of Rusty Wallace's cars to climb inside.
www.bristolmotorspeedway.com
(423) 764-6555

Kingsport, Tennessee

Tennessee's Bright Spot

Tucked away in the Northeast corner of Tennessee, Kingsport is within a day's drive of more than half the nation's population. Kingsport, Tennessee's Bright Spot, is rich in history and scenic splendor. Daniel Boone and Davy Crockett visited the area two centuries ago; and, the area was a popular rest stop for presidents Andrew Jackson, Andrew Johnson and James K. Polk.

Experience the tranquility and excitement of Kingsport, where distractions are only natural. Kingsport – your perfect vacation destination.

Wolves howling at Bays Mountain Park.

Traveler info:
Exit: MP 276.4
For more info:
Kingsport Convention and Visitors Bureau
PO Box 1403
Kingsport, TN 37662
(800) 743-5282
www.kcvb.org

8 *Please refer to map*

structed Fort Watauga. Visit **Carter Mansion** (c. 1775). Outdoor drama, "The Wataugans," is held in July. 1651 West Elk Ave., Elizabethton. (423) 543-5808.

Cross 1882 **Doe River Covered Bridge**, one of Tennessee's oldest covered bridges still in use. Off U.S. 19E, Elizabethton.

Roan Mountain State Park   **6**
1015 Highway 143
Roan Mountain, TN 37687
(423) 772-0190
(800) 250-8620
www.state.tn.us/environment/parks/parks/RoanMtn/
ask.tnstateparks@state.tn.us
•See one of the world's largest displays of Catawba rhododendron

Roan Mountain State Park, beneath its namesake 6,285-foot peak, includes more than 2,000 acres of forestland. The Appalachian Trail can be accessed nearby at Carvers Gap. Naturalist programs plus cabins, skiing and horseback riding are available. Observe the park's diverse wildflowers and wildlife. Atop the mountain is the rhododendron garden, in full bloom about mid-June.

Bristol Area   **7**

Bristol Convention & Visitors Bureau
20 Volunteer Pkwy.,
Bristol, TN 37620
(423) 989-4850
Fax: (423) 989-4867
tourism@bristolchamber.org
www.bristolchamber.org
•Birthplace of Country Music

Bristol, recognized by Congress as the **Birthplace of County Music**, has a rich musical heritage on display at a museum in Bristol Mall (276) 645-0035. The twin cities lie in Virginia and Tennessee, divided by **State Street** with its shops, restaurants and the Paramount Theater (423) 274-8920.

Explore the twin cities'

natural side at **Bristol Caverns**, 1157 Bristol Caverns Hwy., Bristol. (423) 878-2011 or enjoy NASCAR racing at **Bristol Motor Speedway**, (423) 764-6555.

Kingsport Area ❽

Kingsport Convention and Visitors Bureau
151 East Main St.
PO Box 1403
Kingsport, TN 37662
(423) 392-8820
Fax: (423) 392-8803
info@kingsportchamber.com
www.kcvb.org
•Explore Old Stage Road history

COURTESY NETTA

Bays Mountain Park offers barge rides on a 44-acre mountain lake.

Bays Mountain ❽ Park & Planetarium

853 Bays Mountain Park Rd.
Kingsport, TN 37660
(423) 229-9447
Fax: (423) 224-2589
baysmtn@baysmountain.com
www.baysmountain.com
•Explore history and nature

Explore history at the **Netherland Inn and Boatyard** on Holston River, built in the early 1800s as a stop along the Old Stage Road and now a museum. 2144 Netherland Inn Road, Kingsport (423) 246-7982.

Exchange Place, a living history farm on the National Register of Historic Places, six of the eight buildings are original restored structures built 1820-1850. 4812 Orebank Road, Kingsport. (423) 288-6071. See box on page 128 for more information.

Owned by the City of Kingsport, Bays Mountain Park is a 3,000-acre nature preserve with 25 miles of hiking trails, 44-acre lake and nature center/museum with a planetarium. Situated in a natural basin, the park is a haven for wildlife. Includes a raptor center, herpetarium (for snakes), waterfowl aviary and watershed room for native fish and mollusks.

NORTHEAST TENNESSEE SERVICES

GREENEVILLE, TN

Distance: Approx. 65 miles from Parkway • 115 Academy St. • Greeneville, TN 37743 • (423) 638-4111 • Email: kinser@xtn.net

Visit a city rich in historical beauty. The home of President Andrew Johnson and the birthplace of Davy Crockett. Greeneville/ Greene County have been named one of the "Top 25 Mountain Towns 2005" by Pinnacle Living magazine, "The 100 Best Small Towns in America" and "America's Most Charming Towns and Viillages", to name a few.

www.greenecountypartnership.com

Trip Planner Listings

**Blue Ridge/Smoky
Mountains
Ramada Managers
Association**
(800) 2-RAMADA.
ramada.com.
See our ad page 17.

Virtual Blue Ridge
PO Box 1157, Boone,
28607. (828) 265-
4026. freetour.
virtualblueridge.com.

Accommodations

Allstar Lodging
21 Wallace Ave,
Luray 22835.
(540) 843-0606.
Toll-free (866) 780-
7827.
www.allstarlodging.com
Forty different cabins,
cottages, B&Bs.
Kitchens, fireplace,
TV/VCR, hottub, honey-
moon get-away, family
vacation.

Bryce Resort
11 miles west of I-81, exit
273, PO Box 3,
Basye, 22810.
(800) 821-1444.
www.bryceresort.com.

Courtyard by Marriott
1890 Evelyn Byrd Ave.
Harrisonburg, VA 22801.
(540) 432-3031.
www.marriott.com/shdcy
See our ad page 27.

**Hotel Roanoke &
Conference Center**
110 Shenandoah Ave.,
Roanoke, 24016.
(540) 853-8206.
www.hotelroanoke.com.
See our ad page 32.

**Sleep Inn – Tanglewood
Mall**
4045 Electric Rd.,
Roanoke 24014.
(540) 772-1500.
www.dominionlodging.com

Attractions

**Artisans Center
of Virginia**
I-64 Exit 94.
601 Shenandoah Village Dr.,
Waynesboro, 22980.
(540) 946-3294.
www.ArtisansCenterofVirginia.
org.

*Staunton, Va.'s Frontier Culture Museum
offers genuine re-creations of farm life from
the 18th and 19th centuries.*

PAT & CHUCK BLACKLEY

Grand Caverns
5 Grand Caverns Dr.,
Grottoes, 24441.
(888) 430-CAVE.
www.grandcaverns.com.

**Historic Roanoke City
Market**
213 Market St., Roanoke,
24011. (540) 342-2028 X
15.
www.downtownroanoke.org

Frontier Culture Museum
PO Box 810, Staunton,
24401. (540) 332-7850.
www.frontiermuseum.org.
See our ad page 29.

Natural Bridge
US 11 & VA 130, Natural
Bridge, 24578.
(540) 291-2121.
(800) 533-1410.
www.naturalbridgeva.com.
See our ad page 30.

**New Market Battlefield
State Historic Park**
PO Box 1864, New Market,
22844. (540) 740-3101.
www.vmi.edu/museum/nm.

**P. Buckley Moss
Museum**
150 P. Buckley Moss Dr.,
Waynesboro, 22980.
(540) 949-6473.
www.pbuckleymoss.com.
See our ad page 29.

**Virginia Horse
Center**
487 Maury River Rd.,
Lexington, 24450.
(540) 464-2950.
www.horsecenter.org.

**Virginia's Explore
Park**
Milepost 115 Blue
Ridge Parkway,
Roanoke 24014.
(540) 427-1800,
(800) 842-9163.
www.explorepark.org.
See our ad page 30.

Outdoors – Hiking

**Apple Orchard
Falls Trail and Loop**
MP 78.7
Natural Bridge Station
Glenwood Ranger
District.
(540) 291-2188.
www.fs.fed.us/
r8/gwj/ap
7 miles; loop (moderate
to strenuous). The Apple
Orchard Falls (at MP 78.7)
and Cornelius Creek Trails connect with the AT for a loop hike
through the district, which
includes at least 186 miles of
trails.

Humpback Rocks Trails
MP 5.9
(828) 271-4779
www.nps.gov/blri/
humpback.htm
(easy to strenuous). Several
trails from the visitor center
parking lot. Loops and out-and-
backs, including miles of the
AT.

**Otter Creek Recreation
Area**
Between MP 60.6 and 63.6
Amherst County southeast of
Lexington Blue Ridge Parkway,
National Park Service
(434) 299-5125
www.nps.gov/blri
Otter Creek Trail: 3.2 miles;
single trail, MP 60.8. Canal
Lock Trail: .5 miles; single trail.
Trail of the Trees: .5 miles;
loop. Eight miles of trails wind
through the Lake Robertson
State Recreation Area.

**Shenandoah Mountain
Trail**
MP 0

Near Staunton. Deerfield Ranger District, U.S. Forest Service. (540) 885-8028.
www.fs.fed.us/r8/gwj
31 miles; single trail (mostly strenuous). Access from the Mountain House Recreation Area, MP 0 to U.S. 250 west through Staunton. The district's 164,183 acres of land reach into Augusta and Rockbridge counties. Also: the 8-mile Bald Ridge Trail, 14.4 North Mountain Trail and 8-mile Crawford Mountain Trail.

Wild Oak National Recreation Trail
Skyline Drive MP 65.5 to U.S. 33 and Va. 42.
Southwest of Bridgewater Dry River Ranger District, U.S. Forest Service (540) 432-0187
www.fs.fed.us/r8/gwj
26 miles; loop (moderate/strenuous). Access at Todd Lake and North River campgrounds. It visits Little Bald Knob and side trails including the scenic 4.2-mile North River Gorge Trail, is just 26 of the district's 163 miles of trails.

Outdoors – Biking

Blueberry Trail
www.fs.fed.us/r8/gwj
near Ottobine (540) 552-4641
4.1 miles; loop (moderate). Trail starts from the signed trailhead on Va. 742 west of Harrisonburg.

Elizabeth Furnace
near Front Royal
Lee RD (540) 984-4101 or (540)984-4102
www.fs.fed.us/r8/gwj
13.3 miles; loop (difficult) Trail starts at the Elizabeth Furnace Recreation Area.

Massanutten Mountain
near Massanutten visitor center
Rt 211 Lee Hwy (540) 984-4101 or 984-4102
www.fs.fed.us/r8/gwj
50 miles; out and back (moderate). Trail starts at steel gate on Va. 636 at Runkles Gap.

Second Mountain
near Rawley Springs (540) 984-4101 or (540) 984-4102
4.3 miles; out and back (moderate). Trail starts at the intersection of trails on FS 72, six miles uphill from Va. 612.

Sherando Lake Loop
www.fs.fed.us/r8/gwj/gp
near Waynesboro
Glenwood and Pedlar Rd. (540) 291-2188
George Washington and Jefferson NF (540) 265-5100

The summit of Humpback Rocks is a popular spot when the leaves start to turn. MP 6.

JIM WAITE

18.2 miles; loop (moderate to difficult)
Trail starts from the Turkey Pen Trail parking lot off Va. 664 and FS 42.

Restaurants

Belle Grae Inn & Restaurant
www.bellegrae.com
515 W. Frederick St., Staunton, (888) 541-5151, (540) 886-5151. Homemade soups, "creative salads," elegant entrées.

Carlos Brazilian International Restaurant
4167 Electric Rd., Roanoke. (540) 776-1117. Brazilian cuisine.

The Hotel Strasburg
213 S. Holliday St., Strasburg, (540) 465-9191 or (800) 348-8327. Continental cuisine.

Peaks of Otter Lodge
www.peaksofotter.com
PO Box 489, Bedford, 24523 MP 86, (540) 586-1081 or (800) 542-5927. Country buffets.

The Restaurant at Victorian Inn
Woodruff Inns, 138 E. Main, Luray. (540) 743-1494. A Victorian atmosphere.

Retail

Orvis Factory Outlets
31-B Campbell Ave. Roanoke. (540) 344-4520.

VIRGINIA'S JEFFERSON COUNTRY

Accommodations

Holiday Inn University Area & Conference Center
1901 Emmet St., Charlottesville, 22901.
(434)977-7700
www.holiday-inn.com/cho-univarea

Attractions

Monticello
931 Thomas Jefferson Pky., Charlottesville, 22902.
(434) 984-9822.
www.monticello.org. Thomas Jefferson's celebrated mountain-top home. Guided tours daily. Closed Christmas. Adults $13, Children 6-11, $6.

Outdoors – Hiking

Blackwater Creek Trail System
(800)732-5821
(434)847-1811
www.ci.lynchburg.va.us/
Blackwater Creek Bikeway from Ed Page. Entrance to Jefferson Street in downtown Lynchburg
3.1 miles; one-way (easy to moderate). Follow paved trail along abandoned railway. Numerous connecting trails, including a trail through railroad tunnel. Can be hiked or biked.

Crabtree Falls Trail
MP 27.2
Glennwood & Pedlar Ranger District, U.S. Forest Service (540)291-2188
www.fs.fed.us/r8/gwj/
2.9 miles; single trail (moderate to strenuous). 5 miles east of Tye River Gap; Single trail crosses the South Fork Tye River to Crabtree Meadows; hikers can continue another half mile to where it meets the AT.

Old Rag Mountain
Madison County CC & Visitor Center
(540) 948-4455; fax (540) 672-2343
7.2 miles; loop (difficult). 3,000 feet high, Old Rag Mountain, with its solid mass of rugged stones, is perhaps one of the best known and challenging of the peaks in the Blue Ridge.

The Peaks of Otter Lodge looks out onto Abbott Lake and up to Sharp Top and Flat Top peaks.

VICKI ROZEMA

Peaks of Otter Recreation Area Trails
MP 85
Blue Ridge Parkway, National Park Service
(540) 586-4357
www.nps.gov/blri/peaks.htm
Seven trails ranging from easy to strenuous cover 15 miles of geography, including the Fallingwater Cascades, Flat Top and Sharp Top trails, designated national recreation trails. Easiest hikes are around Abbott Lake and on the Johnson Farm Trail.

Outdoors – Biking

Blackwater Creek Bikeway
Lynchburg
(800) 732-5821, (434) 847-1811
www.ci.lynchburg.va.us/
3 miles; one-way (easy to moderate) From Ed Page entrance to Jefferson Street; follows abandoned railway with side trails. Hike or bike.

The Nut
Walnut Creek Park, located off of Va. 631 south of Charlottesville

(434) 296-5844
11 miles of trails, from beginner to expert Trailhead sign with trail map at the park. The Nut is a high-quality, responsibly designed mountain bike park.

Restaurants

Blue Bird Café
625 W. Main St., Charlottesville, (434) 295-1166. American fare with vegetarian options.

Isabella's Italian Trattoria
3225 Old Forest Rd., Lynchburg. (434) 385-1660. Northern Italian cuisine.

Meriwether's Market Restaurant
4925 Boonsboro Rd., Lynchburg. (434) 384-3311. www.meriwethers.com. Casual gourmet restaurant

Metropolitan
214 Water St. Charlottesville. (434) 977-1043. www.metropolitan.wm "New" American cuisine.

Retail

Emerson Creek Pottery
1068 Pottery Ln., Bedford. (540) 297-7884. Factory Direct (866)411-1977 www.emersoncreekpottery.com

Gross' Orchard
6817 Wheats Valley Rd., Bedford (Rt. 640). (540) 586-2436.

Peaks of Otter Winery
2122 Sheep Creek Rd., Bedford (Rt. 680). (540) 586-3707.

River Ridge Mall
3405 Candlers Mountain Rd., Lynchburg. (434) 237-6376.

Spun Earth Pottery
171 Vista Center Dr., Forest. (434) 385-7687.

Virginia Handcrafts
2008 Langhorne Rd., Lynchburg. (434) 846-7029.

Wineries

Afton Mountain Vineyards
Afton. (540) 456-8997. www.aftonmountainvineyards.com.

Barboursville Vineyards & Palladio Restaurant
Barboursville. (540) 832-3824. www.barboursvillewine.com.

Cardinal Point Vineyard & Winery
Afton. (540) 456-8400. www.cardinalpointwinery.com.

DelFosse Vineyards
Faber. (434) 263-6100 www.delfossewine.com.

First Colony Winery
Charlottesville. (877) 979-7105. www.firstcolonywinery.com.

Hill Top Berry Farm & Winery
Nellysford. (434) 361-1266. www.hilltopberrywine.com.

Horton Cellars Winery
Gordonsville. (800) 829-4633. www.hvwine.com.

Jefferson Vineyards
Charlottesville. (800) 272-3042. www.jeffersonvineyards.com.

King Family Vineyard
Crozet. (434) 823-7800. www.kingfamilyvineyards.com.

Kluge Estate Winery and Vineyard and Farm Shop
Charlottesville. (434) 977-3895. www.klugeestate.com.

Hiking

Appalachian National Scenic Trail
Appalachian Trail Conservatory
PO Box 807, Harpers Ferry, WV 25425
(304) 535-6331
www.appalachiantrail.org

The Virginia/North Carolina/Tennessee mountain region is host to about 830 miles (easy to strenuous) of the famed 2,100-plus-mile, Maine-to-Georgia trail. The 540 Virginia miles include one of the trail's prettiest vistas at McAfee Knob near Roanoke. The AT parallels both the Skyline Drive and the Blue Ridge Parkway through Virginia. The 288 North Carolina/Tennessee miles include such favorite sections as Max Patch Bald, Roan Mountain and Clingmans Dome in the Great Smokies. Shelters and campsites are at regular intervals for long-distance hikers; AT often links with shorter trails to allow easier loop or out-and-back dayhikes. Trail access at points throughout the region.

Oakencroft Vineyard & Winery
Charlottesville.
(434) 296-4188.
www.oakencroft.com.

Veritas Winery
Afton.
(540) 456-8000.
www.veritaswines.com.

White Hall Vineyards
White Hall. (434) 823-8615.
www.whitehallvineyards.com.

Wintergreen Winery
Nellysford,
(434) 361-2519.
www.wintergreenwinery.com.

VIRGINIA'S BLUE RIDGE HIGHLANDS

Accommodations

Back Country
P.O. Box 441, Abingdon
24212. (276) 466-4100
www.virginiabackcounrty.com.

Holiday Inn Hotel and Suites
3005 Linden Dr., Bristol
24202. (276) 466-4100.
www.holidayinnandsuites.com.

Inn and Cottages at Orchard Gap
4549 Lightning Ridge Rd.,
Fancy Gap 24328.
(276) 398-3206.
www.bbonline.com/va/orchard gap.

Meadows of Dan Campground
2182 Jeb Stuart Hwy.,
Meadows of Dan, 24120.
(276) 952-2292. www.meadowsofdancampground.com.
RV and tent sites. Bath house, laundry, log cabin rentals. Open year-round.

Mountain Lake Resort
115 Hotel Cir., Pembroke,
24136. (800) 346-3334.
www.mountainlakehotel.com.
See our ad page 53.

Ramada Inn Wytheville
955 Peppers Ferry Rd.,
Wytheville 24382. (276) 228-6000.

Attractions

Birthplace of Country Music Alliance Museum
500 Gate City Hwy., Bristol,
24201. (276) 645-0035.
www.birthplaceofcountrymusic.org.

The Crooked Road
P.O. Box 268, Big Stone Gap,
24219. (866) MTN-MUSIC.
www.thecrookedroad.org. See our ad page 57.

Mabry Mill, at MP 176.2 of the parkway, is the site of a working grist mill as well as summer events.

PAT & CHUCK BLACKLEY

Mountain Lake Resort
115 Hotel Cir., Pembroke,
24136. (800) 346-3334.
www.mountainlakehotel.com.
See our ad page 53.

Outdoors – Hiking

Cascades National Scenic Trail
Blacksburg, (540) 552-4641
www.fs.fed.us/r8/gwj

5 miles over 2 trails; one-way (moderate). Located in the Little Stony Creek Valley, the trail ascends the gorge and culminates at the picturesque 66-foot Cascades Waterfall.

Grayson Highlands State Park
Mouth of Wilson
(276) 579-7092
www.dcr.state.va.us/parks/graysonh.htm

9 scenic trails, none over 2 miles long or of great difficulty. Camping, hiking, picnicking as well as interpretive programs are regular fare at Grayson Highlands.

Mount Rogers National Rec Area
Marion
(800) 628-7202 or
(276) 783-5196
www.southernregion.fs.fed.us/r8/gwj/mr

More than 400 miles of trails. Includes a 58-mile stretch of the Appalachian Trail. Some loops allow hikers to park vehicles, hike for the weekend or a week and return to where they started.

New River Trail State Park
Galax-Pulaski
(276) 699-6778
www.dcr.state.va.us/parks/newriver.htm

57 miles; one-way (easy). 39 miles parallel the New River and following an old abandoned railroad right-of-way.

Rock Castle Gorge Trail
Rocky Knob, MP 167.1
www.nps.gov/blri
10.8 miles; loop (strenuous). Descends 1,800 feet from the Parkway near the Rocky Knob Visitor Center into an area rich in biological diversity.

Virginia Creeper Trail
Abingdon-Whitetop Station
(800) 435-3440 or
(276) 676-2282
www.vacreepertrail.org
33 miles; one-way (easy/moderate). One of Virginia's best recreational trails for bikers, hikers, equestrians and nature lovers. Was once part of a railroad between Abingdon and North Carolina border.

Outdoors – Biking

New River Trail State Park
Galax to Pulaski
(276) 699-6778
www.dcr.state.va.us/parks/new river.htm
57 miles; one-way (easy, easy to moderate) 39 miles parallel the New River and connect Grayson Highlands State Park and the Mt. Rogers NRA. Following an old abandoned railroad right-of-way including bridges and tunnels.

Virginia Creeper Trail
Mount Rogers National
Recreation Area
(276) 783-5196
(800) 628-7202
www.vacreepertrail.com
33 miles; one-way (easy, moderate to easy). One of Virginia's best recreational trails for bikers, hikers, equestrians and nature lovers. Built on railroad between Abingdon and N.C. border.

Restaurants

Doe Run Resort, Inc.
MP 189, (800) 325-6189 or
(276) 398-2212. Friday night
seafood.

Martha Washington Inn
150 W. Main St., Abingdon,
VA (276) 628-9151. Friday
seafood buffet.

The Restaurant at Chateau Morrisette
MP 171.5, Winery Rd.,
PO Box 766, Meadows of Dan
(540) 593-2865. Free-range
meats and poultry.

The Starving Artist Café
134 Wall St. Abingdon (276)
628-8445. Works of local artists.

The Wohlfahrt Haus Restaurant & Dinner Theater
170 Malin Dr., Wytheville.
(888) 950-3382 or
(276) 223-0891. Matterhorn
Restaurant, German flavor.

Retail

Dixie Pottery
17507 Lee Hwy., Abingdon.
(276) 628-5572 or 676-3550.

Fort Chiswell Outlets
731 Factory Merchants Outlet
Dr., Max Meadows, 24360.
(276) 637-6214.
www.ftchiswelloutlets.com.
See our ad page 54.

Mabry Mill & Rocky Knob Cabins
266 Mabry Mill Rd SE.,
Meadows of Dan, 24120.
(276) 952-2947.
www.blueridgeresort.com.
See our ad page 5.

Old Fort Antique Mall
2028 E. Lee Hwy., Wytheville.
(276) 228-4438.
www.antiques-va.com

Winery

Chateau Morrisette
MP 171.5, Winery Rd.,
PO Box 766, Meadows of
Dan, 24120 (540) 593-2865.
www.thedogs.com.

Rail trails make great biking opportunities.

NORTH CAROLINA'S HIGH COUNTRY

Accommodations

Best Western Blue Ridge Plaza
840 E. King St.
(Hwy. 421), Boone, 28607.
(888) 573-0408.
www.bestwesternboone.com.
Indoor pool, game room, FREE deluxe continental breakfast, fireplace/jacuzzi suites.
Microwave, refrigerator in room.

Best Western Eldreth Inn
Hwy US 221 & NC 88
829 E. Main St.,
PO Box 12,
Jefferson, 28640.
(800) 221-8802.
(336)246-8845
www.bestwestern.com/
eldrethinnatmtjefferson.

Cabins on Laurel Creek, LLC
Close to mile marker 249,
Laurel Springs 28644.
(336) 207-7677
www.cabinsonlaurelcreek.com.

Four Seasons at Beech
608 Beech Mountain Pky.,
Beech Mountain, 28604.
(828) 387-4211.
www.4seasons.beech.net.
High atop Beech Mountain,
Four Seasons Lodge offers
unequalled mountain splendor.
Cozy furnishings, warm
hospitality.

Foscoe Realty Rentals
133 Echota Pkwy.,
Boone, NC 28607.
(800)723-7341
www.FoscoeRentals.com

Glendale Springs Inn & Restaurant
7414 Hwy. 16, Glendale
Springs, 28629.
(800) 287-1206.
www.glendalespringsinn.com.
Fine Dining. Between Milepost 258 and 259. Verandas, music, tea. Special occasions. Rooms available year-round.

Highlands at Sugar Resort
2173 Sugar Mountain Dr.,
Banner Elk, 28604.
(828) 898-9601.
www.highlandsatsugar.com

Holiday Inn Express Boone
1943 Blowing Rock, Boone,
28607. (888) 733-6867,
(828) 264-2451. www.
holidayinn-boone.com.
See our ad page 67.

Inn at Yonahlossee
226 Oakley Green, Boone, NC
28607. (828) 963-6400
www.yonahlossee.com.

The Inns of Beech Mountain
700 Beech Mountain Pkwy
Beech Mountain, NC 28604
(866) 284-2770
(828) 387-2252
www.beechalpen.com
see our ad on page 67.

Meadowbrook Inn
Main Street, Blowing Rock,
800/456-5456, 828/295-
4300. www.meadowbrook-
inn.com

Sugar Ski and Country Club
100 Sugar Ski Dr., Banner Elk,
28604. (800) 634-1320.
www.sugarmountain.com.

Switzerland Inn
PO Box 399, Little Switzerland,
28749. (800) 654-4026.
www.switzerlandinn.com. See
our ad page 72.

Willow Valley Resort
354 Bairds Creek Road, Vilas,
28692. (828) 963-6551.
www.willowvalley-resort.com.
Fully furnished cabins, condo's.
Golf, tennis, pool, fireplace.
Three miles south, Boone on
Hwy. 105.

Attractions

Grandfather Mountain
US 221 and the Blue Ridge
Pkwy.(800) 468-7325, (828)
733-4337. www.
grandfather.com. See our ad
page 72.

Linville Caverns
US Hwy-221N
PO Box 567, Marion, 28752.
(800) 419-0540.
www.linvillecaverns.com. See
our ad page 73.

Todd General Store
3866 Railroad Grade Rd.
Todd, NC 28684
(336) 877-1067
www.toddgeneralstore.com

Tweetsie Railroad
PO Box 388, Blowing Rock,
28605. (828) 264-9061.
www.tweetsie.com. See our ad
page 68.

Outdoors – Hiking

Cone and Price Parks Trails
Cone (MP 294); Price (MP 296)
(828) 298-0398
www.nps.gov/blri/conepric.htm
More than 30 miles of loop and
one-way trails in both parks.

Doughton Park Trails
Doughton Park (MP 242.2)
(336) 372-4499
Trail maps: (336) 372-8877
30 miles of one-way and loop
trails. See trail system signboard
at Alligator Back Overlook.

Linn Cove Viaduct Access Trail
Begins at the Linn Cove Visitor
Center MP 304.4. .16 mile; one-
way (easy stroll) Trail travels under-
neath bridge, is handicapped
accessible part of the way.

Linville Falls Trails
MP 316.4, (828) 765-6082
Several trails begin at the Linville
Falls Visitors Center, MP 316.4.
All less than 1 mile Some lead
to the top of the falls, some to
the bottom.

Tanawha Trail
MP 305.5
(800) 438-7500
13.5 miles; one-way (easy to
strenuous). Diverse biological
features. From Julian State Park
to Beacon Heights.
www.ncultra.org

Outdoors – Biking

Junaluska Road Ride
Boone
(800) 438-7500,
(828) 264-1299
www.highcountryhost.com
Begins near top of Howard's
Knob at Junaluska Road in
Watauga County turn off to left.
Swings along Junaluska, con-
nects with Curly Maple Road, to
SR 1323, and back to
Junaluska. Several significant ele-
vation changes. Total elevation
gain: 1,200 ft.

Tweetsie Railroad, operational since 1957, is on the National Register of Historic Places.

GAIL FLEENOR

Railroad Grade Road
Ashe County
(336) 246-9550
www.ashechamber.com
10 miles; easy flat road
Begins at Fleetwood in Ashe
County and runs to Todd. Along
the New River. Ends at Todd
General Store. Access from
N.C. 194 in Todd or U.S. 221
in Flatwood.

Westerly Hills
Beech Mountain
(800) 468-5506)
www.beechmtn.com
10 trails, 18 miles (beginner to
intermediate). Located at the
lower end of the town limits of
Beech Mountain. Last two roads
to the left before the back
entrance to the mountain provide
access. Used for sking and mtn.
biking also.

Westbowl Trails
Beech Mountain
(800) 468-5506
www.beechmtn.com
Five trails (easy,) two mile loop

Restaurants

Bluffs Lodge at Doughton Park
45356 Blue Ridge Pky., Laurel
Springs, 28644.
(336) 372-4499.
www.blueridgeresorts.com. See
our ad page 5.

Manor House Restaurant at Chetola Resort
North Main Street, Blowing
Rock, (828)395-5505.
(800)243-8652
Mountain delicacies.
www.chetola.com

Mast Farm Inn Restaurant
2543 Broadstone Rd., Valle
Crucis, 888/963-5857,
828/963-5857. Fresh organic,
contemporary regional cuisine.

Shatley Springs Inn
407 Shatley Springs Rd.,
Crumpler, 336/982-2236.
"Country cooking" served family
style.

Retail

DeWoolfson Down, Inc.
9452 Hwy. 105, Banner Elk,
28604. (800) 833-3696.
www.dewoolfsondown.com.
See our ad page 69.

Doe Ridge Pottery
137 W. King St., Boone,
28607. (828) 264-1127.
www.doeridgepottery.com.

Mast General Store
Highway 194, Valle Crucis,
28691. (828) 963-6511.
www.mastgeneralstore.com. See
our ad page 70.

Tanger Outlet Center
a.k.a. Shoppes on the Parkway
at Blowing Rock.
(828) 295-4444.
www.tangeroutlet.com

Tanner Factory Outlet
Hwy 1321 Bypass
PO Box 1209, Blowing Rock.
(828) 295-7031.

Biking

TransAmerica Bicycle Route
Adventure Cycling
Association
PO Box 8308,
Missoula, MT 59807
(406) 721-1776,
(800) 755-2453
www.adv-cycling.org

The TransAmerica Bicycle
Route, enters Virginia at
Breaks Interstate Park in the
Blue Ridge Highlands. It
runs northeast from there, all
on public roads,   to enter
Catawba. After leaving
Rockbridge County, it climbs
to the Parkway at MP 27.2
and drops to Rockfish Gap
(Parkway MP 0), to travel on
out of the Blue Ridge
region.

NORTH CAROLINA'S BLUE RIDGE/ASHEVILLE

Accommodations

Comfort Suites-Biltmore Square Mall
890 Brevard Rd., Asheville, 28806. (800) 622-4005, (828)655-4000. www.ashevillenccomfort.com.

Fairfields Mountains Resort
747 Buffalo Creek Rd., Lake Lure, 28746. (800) 829-3149. www.fairfieldmountains.com. See our ad page 82.

Fox Run Townhouses & Fairways of the Mountains
180 Herman Wilson Road Lake Lure, 28746 (866) 4MY-VACATION www.8664myvacation.com See our ad page 84.

The Grove Park Inn Resort & Spa
290 Macon Ave., Asheville, 28804. (800) 438-5800. www.groveparkinn.com. See our ad page 89.

Haywood Park Hotel
One Battery Park Ave. Asheville 28801 (828) 252-2522 www.lakelure.com See our ad page 92.

Mill House Lodge
1150 West Blue Ridge Rd. PO Box 309, Flat Rock, 28731. (800) 736-6073. www.millhouselodge.com. See our ad page 85.

Premier Properties Lake Country Real Estate
2992 Memorial Hwy., Lake Lure, 28746. (800) 742-9556. www.LakeCountryNC.com/brtg. See our ad page 83.

Attractions

Biltmore Estate
One Approach Rd., Asheville, 28803. (800) 411-3812. www.biltmore.com. See our ad page 90.

Chimney Rock Park
PO Box 39, Chimney Rock, 28720. (800) 277-9611. www.chimneyrockpark.com. See our ad page 82.

Cradle of Forestry
Hwy 276-Pisgah Hwy., Pisgah Forest, 28768. (828) 877-3130. www.cradleofforestry.com. See our ad page 92.

Handmade pottery and other craft products are available at shops throughout the region.

VICKIE ROZEMA

Folk Art Center
Milepost 382 BRP, Asheville, 28815. (828) 298-7928. www.southernhighlandguild.org. See our ad page 91.

Lake Lure Tours, Beach & Marina
2930 Memorial Hwy./Hwy. 64/74A, PO Box 541, Lake Lure, 28746. (877) FUN-4-ALL (386-4255). www.lakelure.com. See our ad page 83.

Restaurants

Bridge Street Café and Inn
145 Bridge St., Hot Springs, (828) 622-0002.

Natural and organic Mediterranean cuisine.

Chimney Rock Park's Old Rock Café
US 64/74A, Chimney Rock, (828) 625-2329, (800) 277-9611. Indoor/outdoor dining.

The Gables Restaurant at Mary Mills Coxe Inn
1210 Greenville Hwy., Hendersonville, (828) 692-5900, (800) 230-6541. American and International cuisine.

Nu Wray Inn Restaurant
Town Square, Burnsville, (828) 682-2329, (800) 368-9729. Fine dining.

Red Rocker Inn Restaurant
136 N. Dougherty St., Black Mountain, (828) 669-5991, (888) 669-5991.

Tupelo Honey Café
12 College St., Asheville, (828) 255-4863. Southern home cooking with an uptown twist. Breafast all day.

Retail

Bellagio
5 Biltmore Plaza, Asheville, 28803. (828) 277-8100. www.bellagioarttowear.com

Blue Spiral 1
38 Biltmore Ave., Asheville, 28801. (828) 251-0202. www.bluespiral1.com

BonWorth Factory Outlet
40 Francis Rd., Hendersonville. (828) 692-0658. www.bonworth.com

Crabtree Meadows Gift Shop
PO Box 175, Little Switzerland, 28749. (282) 675-4236. www.blueridgeresorts.com. See our ad page 5.

Foam & Fabric Outlet
3049 Hendersonville Hwy., Fletcher. (828) 684-0801.

Manual Woodworkers & Weavers
U.S. 74, Bat Cave. (828) 625-9523.

Parris Shoe World
Sugarloaf Rd., Hendersonville. (828) 697-6140.

Tanner Factory Store
Fashion Circle off of Rock Rd., Rutherfordton. (828) 287-3637.

World of Clothing
135 Sugarloaf Rd., Hendersonville. (828) 693-4131.

Services

Handmade in America
PO Box 2089, Asheville 28802. (800) 331-4154. www.handmadeinamerica.org. See our ad page 91.

NORTH CAROLINA SMOKIES

Accommodations

Bryson City Fryemont Inn
245 Fryemont St., Bryson City, NC 28713. (800) 845-4879. (828)488-2159 www.fryemontinn.com.

Cataloochee Ranch
119 Ranch Dr., Maggie Valley, 28751. (800) 868-1401, (828) 926-1401. www.cataloocheeranch.com.

Great Smoky Real Estate
2779 Soco Rd., Maggie Valley, NC 28751. (866) 811-4640. www.greatsmokyrentals.com. See our ad page 101.

Highlands Suite Hotel & Mountain High Lodge
Mountain High Lodge: 200 Main St., Highlands 28741. (877) 553-4801.

Highlands Suite Hotel: 205 Main St., Highlands 28741. (877) 530-2835. www.mountainhighinn.com, www.highlandsuitehotel.com. See our ad page 101.

Nantahala Cabins

580 Nantahala Cabins Ln., Bryson City, 28713. (877) 488-1622. www.nantahalacabins.com.

Ramada Limited Cherokee

196 Painttown Road, Cherokee, 28719. (800) 849-5263. www.cherokeeramada.com.

The Southern Appalachians' mysterious balds make for great hiking and backpacking.

JERRY WHALEY

Attractions

The Cherokee Indian Reservation

PO Box 460-124, Cherokee, 28719. (800) 438-1601. www.cherokee-nc.com. See our ad page104.

Great Smoky Mtns Railroad

119 Front St., PO Box 397, Dillsboro, 28725. (800) 872-4681 ext. BF. www.gsmr.com. See our ad page102.

Harrah's Cherokee Casino

777 Casino Dr., Cherokee, 28719. (800) HARRAHS (427-7247). www.harrahs.com. See our ad page 103.

T. Pennington Art Gallery

Two Locations: 15 N. Main St., Waynesville, 28786 & 1179 Main St., Blowing Rock, 28605 (828) 452-9284. www.tpennington.com. See our ad page100.

Outdoors – Hiking

Appalachian Trail to Wesser Bald

Wesser Gap (800) 432-4678 www.ncguide.com/outdoors/hiking.htm.2 miles; one-way (moderate).Scenic portion of Appalachian Trail; perfect for day hikes. Trailhead is at Wesser Gap.

Great Smoky Mountains

National Park Trails Oconaluftee Visitor's Center Cherokee, NC (828) 497-1900 www.nps.gov/grsm More than 800 miles of trails, including Abrams Falls, Alum Cave Bluff Trail, Rainbow Falls Trail, and Old Settlers Trail. Cherokee, NC (828) 497-1900

Joyce Kilmer Memorial Trail

Joyce Kilmer Memorial Forest (800) 432-4678 www.main.nc.us/graham/hiking/joycekil.html 2 miles; loop (easy) Last remnant of virgin forest in the Southern Appalachians Trailhead is in Joyce Kilmer Forest parking lot.

Nantahala National Forest Trails

Wayah Ranger District, Sloan Road Franklin, NC 28734 (800) 432-4678 A great variety of scenic trails, including miles of the Appalachian Trail. Difficulty ranging from easy to strenuous. Loops and one-ways.

Trails to Waterfalls

Smoky Mountains region (800) 432-4678 www.visitsmokies.org Great walks to Bridal Veil, Dry, Cullasajah, Looking Glass, Whitewaer and other Smokies' area falls.

Outdoors – Biking

Cataloochee Valley

Southeast corner of Great Smoky Mountains National Park (865) 436-1200 www.nps.gov/grsm Biking trails run through what was once the largest settlement in the Smokies. Junction of I-40 and U.S. 276.

Great Smoky Mountains

National Park (865) 436-1200 www.nps.gov/grsm Biking is allowed on park roads that are open to vehicular traffic. Bikes prohibited on park trails, except for Cades Cove Loop Rd., Greenbrier and Treemont Rds. in TN. Lakeview Dr.,Cataloochee Valley in NC.

Tsali Recreation Area Trails

Fontana Lake (828) 479-6431 www.mtbikewnc.com Fontana Lake area in the Nantahala National Forest 11.9 miles; easy, fast. 4 main trails; great views.

Restaurants

Dillsboro Steak & Seafood House

489 Haywood Rd., Dillsboro, (828) 586-8934. Fresh seafood.

Lulu's Café

612 W. Main St., Sylva. (828) 586-8989. From Tropical Pork Tenderloins to Walnut Spinach Ravioli.

Nantahala Village Mountain Resort

9400 Hwy. 19W, Bryson City. (800) 438-1507, (828) 488-2826. Casually elegant atmosphere. Everything from Fried Chicken to Eggs Benedict, with a nightly vegetarian meal. www.nvnc.com

Randolph House Country Inn

Opens May 1st. 223 Fryemont Rd., Bryson City, 28713. (800) 480-3472, (828) 488-3472. Southern gourmet dining.

Retail

Barclay Factory Outlet

190 Everett St., Bryson City. (828) 488-8020.

Coast Lamp Factory Outlet

35 Church St., Canton (828) 648-7876, (800) 635-1208

Tanner Outlet

Holly Springs Plaza, Franklin. (828) 524-8683.

Thad Woods Factory Outlet

227 Muse Business Park, Waynesville. (828) 452-3789.

TENNESSEE SMOKIES

Accommodations

Caney Creek Cabins

792 Caney Creek Rd., Pigeon Forge, 37863. (800) 273-5116. www.caneycreek.com.

Chalet Village Properties

1441 Wiley Oakley Dr., Gatlinburg, 37738. (800) 722-9617. www.chaletvillage.com. See our ad page 111.

Cove Mountain Resort
3202 Wears Valley Rd.,
Sevierville, 37862.
(800) 559-5325.
www.covemountain.com.
See our ad page 118.

Gatlinburg Real Estate & Rentals
211 Parkway, Gatlinburg,
37738. (800) 359-1661.
www.gatlinburgchalets.com.

The Lodge at Buckberry Creek
961 Campbell Lead Rd.,
Gatlinburg 37738.
(866) 30-LODGE.
www.buckberrylodge.com.
See our ad page 113.

Mountain Laurel Chalets
440 Ski Mountain Rd.,
Gatlinburg, 37738.
(800) 784-6532,
(865) 436-5277.
www.mtnlaurelchalets.com.

Oak Square at Gatlinburg
685 River Rd., Gatlinburg
37738. (865)436-7582.
www.oaksquare.net.
www.scenicviewrentals.com

Pigeon Forge Best Westerns
Plaza Inn
3755 Parkway Pigeon Forge,
37863
(800) 232-5656
www.bestwesternplazainn.com

Best Western Toni Inn
3810 Parkway Pigeon Forge,
37863
(800) 422-3232
www.bestwesterntoniinn.com
See our ad on page 116

Ramada Inn of Cumberland Gap
US 25 E. Hwy 58, Cumberland
Gap 37724. (423) 869-3637.
www.cumberlandgap-ramada.com

Ramada Inn & Convention Center
4014 Parkway, Pigeon Forge
37863. (800) 523-3919.
www.smokymountainresorts.com

Ramada Inn Four Seasons
576 Parkway, Gatlinburg
37738. (865) 436-5348.
www.reaganresorts.com

Ramada Limited
3385 Winfield Dunn Pkwy., PO
Box 250, Kodak 37764. (800)
348-4652.
www.ramadalimitedkodak.com

Ramada Limited - East
722 Brakebill Rd., Knoxville
37924. (865) 546-7271.
www.theramada.com/
knoxville02543.

Cataloochee Cove is a classic swimmin' hole.

Ramada Limited Music Road Area
2193 Parkway, Pigeon Forge
37863. (800) 269-1222.
www.pigeonforgeramada.com/
brptg.

Ramada Limited Suites
239 Dollywood Ln., Pigeon
Forge 37863. (800) 523-
3916.
www.smokymountainresorts.
com.

Reagan Resorts
Gatlinburg
reaganresorts@aol.com
www.reaganresorts.com. See
our ad page 147.

Resort Quest Smoky Mountains
718 Golf View Blvd., Pigeon
Forge, 37863.
(888) 255-8343. www.
resortquestsmokymountains.com.
See our ad page 117.

Tennessee Overhill
PO Box 143, 727 Tennessee
Ave., Etowah 37331. (423)
263-7232.
www.tennesseeoverhill.com.

Attractions

Forbidden Caverns
455 Blowing Cave Rd,
Sevierville, 37876. (865) 453-
5972.
www.forbiddencaverns.com

Lost Sea
140 Lost Sea Rd., Sweetwater,
37874. (865) 337-6616.
www.thelostsea.com.

Outdoors – Hiking

Alum Cave Bluff
To Mount LeConte, between
Newfound Gap and Chimney
Tops. (865) 436-1200
www.nps.gov/grsm

4.4-mile; round-trip (moderate).
Past creeks and scenic overlooks.

Boulevard Trail
Take the Appalachian Trail from
Newfound Gap
(865) 436-1200
www.localhikes.com
16-mile; round-trip. The easiest
and most popular of the five
trails to the summit of Mount
LeConte.

Laurel Falls Trail
South end of Gatlinburg
(865) 436-1200
www.nps.gov/grsm

One of the easiest; 2.5
roundtrip. Waterfall is 60 feet
high.

Sugarlands Valley Nature Trail
Gatlinburg
(865) 436-1200
www.nps.gov/grsm
3,000-foot; loop trail.
Educational exhibits paved to
accommodate visitors with dis-
abilities. Trailhead is located off
Newfound Gap Road, one-quar-
ter mile south of Sugarlands
Visitor Center.

Outdoors – Biking

Cades Cove Loop Road
Cades Cove
11-mile road off U.S. 321
(865) 436-1200
www.nps.gov/grsmgsmsite/cad
escove.html
Closed to automobile traffic on
Wednesday and Saturday until
10 a.m. from spring through
mid-September to allow a
leisurely cycle around the valley.
Bicycles can be rented at the
Cades Cove Campground
store.

Cherokee Park
Morristown
(423) 586-5232
Camping and water recreation.
Begin cycling anywhere in park.

Foothills Parkway
Great Smoky Mountains
National Park
(865) 436-1200
www.nps.gov/grsm/gsmsite/
peaks.html#foothills
The parkway skirts the northern
side of the Smokies. West section runs 20 miles from Walland
to Chilhowee; east section
begins at Cosby (I-40); The Spur
follows the west prong of the
Little Pigeon River.

Restaurants

Altruda's Italian Restaurant
The Commons, 125 N. Peters
Rd. at Kingston Pike, Knoxville.
(865) 690-6144. Italian restaurant.

Buckhorn Inn
2140 Tudor Mountain Rd.,
Gatlinburg. (865) 436-4668.
Fixed price breakfast and dinner
with gourmet entrée.

Old Mill Restaurant
160 Old Mill Ave., Pigeon
Forge. (865) 453-4628 or
(888) 453-6455. Southern-style
cooking. www.old-mill.com
See our ad page 118

The Park Grill
1110 Parkway, Gatlinburg,
37738. (865) 436-2300.
www.peddlerparkgrill.com.

Regas
318 N. Gay St., Knoxville.
(865) 63-REGAS. A Knoxville
icon in downtown.

Retail

Belz Factory Outlet World
2655 Teaster Ln., Pigeon Forge.
(865) 453-7316.

Christmas Place
PO Box 958
2470 Parkway, Pigeon Forge,
37863. (800) 445-3396.
www.christmasplace.com. SSee
our ad page 117.

Great Smoky Arts & Crafts Community
PO Box 807, Gatlinburg,
37738. (865) 436-4315.
www.artsandcraftscommunity.
com. See our ad page 111.

The Old Mill Square
175 Old Mill Ave., Pigeon
Forge, 37863.
(865) 453-1104.
www.old-mill.com. See our ad
page 118.

Pigeon Forge Factory Outlet Mall
2850 Parkway, Pigeon Forge.
(865) 428-2828.

Tanger Outlet Center
161 E. Wears Valley Rd.,
Pigeon Forge. (865) 428-7002.

Tanger Outlet Center at Five Oaks
1645 Parkway, Sevierville.
(865) 453-1053.

Accommodations

Ramada Inn Kingsport
2005 LaMasa Dr. Kingsport, TN
37660 (800) 2-RAMADA

Camping is just one of the outdoor pleasures in the Blue Ridge.

KEN DUNN

(423) 245-0271
www.kinsportramada.com

Travelers Inn
505 West Elk Ave., Elizabethton
37643. (423) 543-3344.

Outdoors – Hiking

Backbone Rock Rec Area Trails
Shady Valley Trail. Also falls
loop of 3.8 miles and 2.4-mile
loop. (423) 735-1500
2.2 miles; one-way (moderate).
Leads to Appalachian Trail.

Davy Crockett Birthplace Trails
Limestone
(423) 257-2167
www.state.tn.us/environment/
parks/parks/DavyCrockettSHP
3/4 hour; loop (easy). Starts at
campground; goes along the
Nolichucky.

Jacobs Creek Rec Area Trails
Bristol
(423) 735-1500
3 miles; one-way (easy). Follows
lake.

Roan Mountain Trails
(423) 772-0190 (800)250-
8620
www.state.tn.us/environment/
parks/parks/RoanMtn
8 trails, 12 miles of trails;
2.25 mtn. bike trails, one-way
(easy to strenuous). Trailheads all
throughout the park.

Sycamore Shoals Trails
Elizabethton
(423) 543-5808
www.state.tn.us/environment/
parks/parks/SycamoreShoals
2 miles; one-way/loop (easy).
Walking/fitness trail.

Outdoors – Biking

Bays Mountain Park & Planetarium
Kingsport
(423) 229-9447

www.baysmountain.com
Only approved mountain bikes
permitted.

Warriors' Path Trails
Kingsport
(423) 239-8531

www.state.tn.us/environment/
parks/parks/WarriorsPath/

4 miles of mountain bike trails
available; biking also on park
roads.

Restaurants

The Firehouse Restaurant
627 W. Walnut St., Johnson
City. (423) 929-7377.
Hickory-smoked barbecue specialties.

The Parsons Table
100 W. Woodrow Ave.,
Jonesborough, (423) 753-
8002. An 1870s converted
church.

Ridgewood Barbecue, LLC
900 Elizabethton Hwy., Bluff
City. (423) 538-7543. The
area's oldest and most well-
known barbecue restaurant.

Skoby's
1001 Konnarock Rd., Kingsport.
(423) 245-2761. Crab-stuffed
orange roughy and Applewood-
Jack Daniels Baby Back Ribs.

Troutdale Dining Room
412 Sixth St., Bristol, TN.
(423) 968-9099. Dine in a historic home on International and
American cuisine.

Retail

Factory Stores of America
354 Shadowtown Rd. (Tenn.
126), Blountville. (423) 323-
4419 (800) SHOP-USA.

Visitor Centers and Other Sources for More Information

VIRGINIA'S SHENANDOAH VALLEY

Travel Association
277 W. Old Cross Rd.
New Market, VA
22844-1040
(540) 740-3132
www.shenandoah.org

Blue Ridge Parkway Visitor Center at Explore Park
Parkway MP 115, PO Box 8508
Roanoke, VA 24014
(540) 427-1800
(800) 842-9163
www.explorepark.org

Front Royal-Warren County Visitors Center
414 E. Main St.
Front Royal, VA 22630
(800) 338-2576
(540) 635-5788
www.frontroyalchamber.com

Harrisonburg/ Rockingham County
10 E. Gay St.
Harrisonburg, VA 22802
(540) 434-2319
www.hrcvb.com
See our ad page 27.

Jefferson County Convention and Visitors Bureau
PO Box A, Harpers Ferry, WV 25425
(866) HELLO-WV.
www.hello-wv.com.
See our ad page 21.

Lexington-Rockbridge County Visitors Center
106 E. Washington St
Lexington, VA 24450
(877) 453-9822
(540) 463-3777
www.lexingtonvirginia.com

Luray-Page County CoC
46 E. Main St.
Luray, VA 22835
(540) 743-3915,
(888) 743-3915
www.luraypage.com

Roanoke Valley Visitor Information Center
101Shenandoah Ave.,NE
Roanoke, VA 24016
(800) 635-5535, (540) 345-8622, (540) 342-6025
www.visitroanokeva.com
See our ad page 31.

Staunton-Augusta County Travel Information Center
1250 Richmond Rd.
Staunton, VA 24402-0810
(800) 332-5219
(540) 332-3927
www.stauntonva.org

Rockfish Gap Info Center
20 Afton Circle
Waynesboro, VA 22920
(540) 943-5187
www.augustachamber.org

Waynesboro Office of Tourism
PO Box 1028
Waynesboro, VA 22980
(866) 53-1957
(540) 942-6644
www.waynesboro.va.us
See our ad page 28

Winchester-Frederick County CVB
1360 S. Pleasant Valley Rd.
Winchester, VA 22601
(800) 662-1360
(540) 542-1326
www.winchesterva.org

VIRGINIA'S JEFFERSON COUNTRY

Bedford CoC
305 E. Main St.
Bedford, VA 24523
(800) 933-9535
(540) 586-9401
www.visitbedford.com

Bedford Welcome Center
816 Burks Hill Rd., Bedford 24523. (540) 587-5681,
(877) HI-PEAKS.
www.visitbedford.com
See our ad page 44.

Charlottesville/Albemarle CVB
Rt. 20 S, PO Box 172
Charlottesville, VA 22902
(877) 386-1102
(434) 293-6789
soveryvirginia.org
See our ad page 41.

Lynchburg Regional CVB
216 12th St.
Lynchburg, VA 24501
(434)847-1811
www.discoverlynchburg.org
See our ad page 43.

Nelson County Convention and Visitors Bureau
8519 Thomas Nelson Hwy.
Lovingston, VA 22949
(800) 282-8223
(434) 263-7015
www.nelsoncounty.com
See our ad page 45.

Orange County Visitors Center
PO Box 133
Orange, VA 22960
(540) 672-1653
www.visitocva.com

Smith Mountain Lake CoC/Partnership
16430 Booker T. Washington Hwy. Unit #2, Moneta, VA 24121
(800) 676-8203
(540) 721-1203
www.visitsmithmountainlake.com

VIRGINIA'S BLUE RIDGE HIGHLANDS

Abingdon CVB
335 Cummings St.
Abingdon, VA 24210
(276) 676-2282,
(800) 435-3440
www.abingdon.com/tourism

Carroll County Office of Tourism
605-I Pine St., Hillsville
24343. (276) 730-3100.
www.ChillsNet.org.
See our ad page 53.

Floyd County CoC
PO Box 510, Floyd, VA 24091
(540) 745-4407
www.visitfloyd.org

Franklin CoC
261 Franklin St.
Rocky Mount, VA 24151
(540) 483-9542
www.franklincountyva.org

City of Galax
111 E. Grayson
Galax, VA 24333
(276) 238-8130
www.visitgalax.com

Grayson County Tourist Information
107 East Main St.
Independence, 24348
(276) 773-3711.
www.graysoncountyva.com

Patrick County CoC
PO Box 577, Stuart, VA 24171
(276) 694-6012

Pulaski County CoC
4440 Cleburne Blvd.
Ste. B, Dublin, VA 24084
(540) 674-1991
www.swva.net/ pulaskichamber

Town of Rocky Mount
345 Donald Ave.
Rocky Mount, VA 24151
(540) 483-0907
www.rockymountVA.org

Visitor Centers and Other Sources for More Information

Southwest Highlands Regional Visitors Center
975 Tazewell St.
Wytheville, VA 24382
(800) 446-9670
www.virginiablueridge.org

Smyth Chamber of Commerce
214 West Main Suite E.
Marion, 24354
(276) 783-3161.
www.smythchamber.org

Wytheville Area CVB
150 E. Monroe St.
Wytheville, VA 24382
(877) 347-8307
(276)223-3355
www.visitwytheville.com
See our ad page 55.

N.C. High Country Host Visitor Center
1700 Blowing Rock Rd.
Boone, NC 28607
(800) 438-7500
(828) 264-1299
www.highcountryhost.com

Alleghany CoC
58 S. Main St.
Sparta, NC 28675
(800) 372-5473
(336) 372-5473
www.sparta-nc.com

Ashe CoC
6 N. Jefferson Ave.
West Jefferson, NC 28694
(336) 246-9550
(888) 343-2743
www.ashechamber.com

Avery/Banner Elk CoC
2 Shoppes of Tynecastle
Banner Elk, NC 28604
(800) 972-2183
(828) 898-5605
www.banner-elk.com

Beech Mountain CoC
403-A Beech Mountain Pkwy.
Beech Mountain, NC 28604
(800) 468-5506
(828) 387-9283
www.beechmtn.com
See our ad page 71.

Blowing Rock CoC
132 Park Ave.
Blowing Rock, NC 28605
(800) 295-7851
(828) 295-7851
www.blowingrock.com

Boone Area CoC
208 Howard St.
Boone, NC 28607
(800) 852-9506
(828) 264-2225
www.boonechamber.com
See our ad page 69.

Mitchell County Visitors Center
79 Parkway Rd.
Spruce Pine, NC 28777
(800) 227-3912
(828) 765-9483
www.mitchell-county.com

Wilkes County CoC
717 Main St.
N. Wilkesboro, NC 28659
(336) 838-8662
www.wilkesnc.org

Asheville/Buncombe Co. CVB
PO Box 1010
Asheville, NC 28802
(828) 258-6101
(800) 257-5583
www.ashevillechamber.org
See our ad page 87.

Black Mountain/ Swannanoa CoC
201 E. State St.
Black Mountain, NC 28711
(828) 669-2300
(800) 669-2301
www.blackmountain.org
See our ad page 85.

Brevard CoC
35 W. Main St.
Brevard, NC 28712
(828) 883-3700
(800) 648-4523
www.brevardncchamber.org

Burke County Travel and Tourism Commission
102 E. Union St.
Courthouse Square,
Morganton, NC 28655
(828) 433-6793
(888) 462-2921
www.hci.net/~bcttc

Henderson County Travel and Tourism
201 S. Main St.
Hendersonville, NC 28792
(800) 828-4244
www.historichendersonville.org

Hickory Nut Gorge Visitors Center
PO Box 32
Chimney Rock, NC 28720
(828) 625-2725
www.chimney-rock.com/ chamber

Madison County Visitors Center
72 S. Main St.
Mars Hill, NC 28754
(828) 680-9031
(877) 262-3476
www.madisoncounty-nc.com

McDowell County
1170 W. Tate St.
Marion, NC 28752
(828) 652-1103
(888) 233-6111
www.mcdowellnc.org

Rutherford County TDA
1990 U.S. 221 South
Forest City, NC 28043
(800) 849-5998
www.rutherfordtourism.com
See our ad page 81.

Transylvania County TDA
35 W. Main St.
Brevard, NC 28712
(800) 648-4523
(828) 883-8550
www.visitwaterfalls.com

Yancey County CoC
106 W. Main St.
Burnsville, NC 28714
(828) 682-7413
(800) 948-1632
www.yanceychamber.com

Smoky Mountain Host of N.C.
4437 Georgia Rd.
Franklin, NC 28734
(800) 432-4678
www.visitsmokies.org

Cherokee Welcome Center
PO Box 460
Cherokee, NC 28719
(800) 438-1601
www.cherokee-nc.com

Cashiers CoC
PO Box 238
Cashiers, NC 28717
(828) 743-5941
www.cashiers-nc.com

Cherokee County Chamber of Commerce
805 West US 64
Murphy, NC 28906
(828) 837-2242.
www.cherokeecountychamber .com. Two hours from any-where, but only one step from heaven. Experience Cherokee County.

Franklin CoC
425 Porter St.
Franklin, NC 28734
(828) 524-3161
(866) 372-5546
(800) 336-7829
www.franklin-chamber.com

Visitor Centers and Other Sources for More Information

Graham County CoC
PO Box 1206
427 Rodney Orr Bypass
Robbinsville, NC 28771
(828) 479-3790
(800) 470-3709
www.grahamchamber.com

Maggie Valley CoC and Visitor's Bureau
2487 Soco Rd.
Maggie Valley, NC 28751
(828) 926-1686
(800) 624-4431
www.maggievalley.com

Haywood County TDA
1233 N. Main St.
Waynesville, NC 28786
(800) 334-9036, (828) 452-0152
www.smokeymountains.net/brp See our ad page 99.

Haywood County CoC
73 Walnut St.
PO Drawer 600
Waynesville, NC 28786
(828) 456-3021
(877) 456-3073
www.haywood-nc.com

Andrews CoC
First and Locust St.
Andrews, NC, 28901
(828) 321-3584
www.grove.net/~andrewschamber

Clay County CoC
388 U.S. 64 Business
Hayesville, NC 28904
(828) 389-3704
www.claycounty-nc-chamber.com

Highlands Area CoC & Visitor Center
Highlands, NC 28741
(828) 526-2112
www.highlands-chamber.com

Jackson County CoC
773 W. Main St.
Sylva, NC 28779
(828) 586-2155
(800) 962-1911
www.nc-mountains.com

Swain County CoC
16 Everett St.
Bryson City, NC 28713
(828) 488-3681
(800) 867-9246
www.greatsmokies.com

Town of Dillsboro
42 Front St.
Dillsboro, NC 28725
(828) 586-1439
www.visitdillsboro.org

TENNESSEE SMOKIES

Gatlinburg Welcome Center
U.S. 441 between Gatlinburg & Pigeon Forge
(865) 436-0519
(800) 568-4748
www.gatlinburgtennessee.com

Great Smoky Mountains Assoc.
115 Park Headquarters Rd.
Gatlinburg, 37738
Stop at Oconaluftee Visitor Center at Great Smokies Park entrance. (888) 898-9102.
www.smokiesstore.org.

Loudon County Visitors Bureau
1075 Hwy. 321 N., I-75, exit 81
Lenoir City, TN 37771
(888) 568-3662
(865) 986-6822

Middle East Tennessee Tourism Council
10205 South River Trail
Knoxville, TN 37922
(800) 440-0447
(865) 777-2606
www.VacationEastTennessee.org

Oak Ridge Welcome Center
302 S. Tulane Ave.
Oak Ridge, TN 37830-6726
(865) 482-7821
(800) 887-3429
www.visit-or.org

Pigeon Forge Welcome Center
2450 Parkway
(865) 453-8574,
(800) 251-9100
www.mypigeonforge.com
See our ad page 115.

Smoky Mountain Visitors Bureau
7906 E. Lamar Alexander Pkwy., Townsend 37882.
(865)448-6134.
www.smokymountains.org.

Tennessee Overhill Heritage Association
PO Box 143
Etowah, TN 37331
(423) 263-7232
www.tennesseeoverhill.com

Townsend Visitors Center
7906 E. Lamar Alexander Pkwy.
Townsend, TN 37882
(865) 448-6134
(800) 525-6834
www.blountweb.com/townsend/visitorsctr.htm

NORTHEAST TENNESSEE

Northeast Tennessee Tourism Association
PO Box 415
Jonesborough, TN 37659
(423) 913-5550
(800) 468-6882
www.netta.com

Bristol CVB
20 Volunteer Pkwy./PO Box 519
Bristol, VA/TN 24203-0519
(423) 989-4850
www.bristolchamber.org

Elizabethton/Carter Co. CoC Tourism Council
500 Veteran Memorial Pkwy.
PO Box 190
Elizabethton, TN 37644-0190
(423) 547-3850
www.tourelizabethton.com

Greene County Partnership Tourism Council
115 Academy St., Ste. 1
Greeneville, TN 37743
(423) 638-4111
www.greenecountypartnership.com

Johnson City CVB
603 E. Market St.,
Johnson City, TN 37605-0180
(800) 852-3392 ext. BR
www.visitjohnsoncitytn.com
See our ad page 127.

Kingsport CVB
151 E. Main St., PO Box 1403
Kingsport, TN 37662-1403
(423) 392-8820
(800) 743-5282
www.kingsportchamber.org
See our ad page 128.

Unicoi County CoC
100 S. Main Ave., PO Box 713
Erwin, TN 37650-0713
(423) 743-3000
www.unicoicounty.org

FOR EVEN MORE
www.blueridgeparkwayusa.com
INFORMATION

Index

Index

Bloom Calendar
···

T he bloom peak occurs within the dates indicated. Bloom peaks along
  the Parkway in Virginia are usually earlier than in North Carolina due
to lower elevation. The selected locations are referenced to Parkway milepost markers. The letters PA represent picnic areas.

Flowers	Peak Bloom	Milepost Location
Mayapple	Mar-Apr	76.2-76.4, 296-297, 315-317, 320.8, 339.5
Serviceberry-Sarvis	Mar-May	241-242, 294-297, 308.3, 347.6, 368-370
Bird-Foot Violet	Mar-May	147.4, 202, 260.5, 379
Tulip Poplar	Apr-May	Common in low woods and coves
Soloman's Seal	Apr-May	Common on moist wooded slopes, coves
Fringed Phacelia	Apr-May	370-375
Bloodroot	Apr-May	85.6, 191-193, 198.7, 294
Trillium	Apr-May	175, 200-216, 339-340, 364.6
Redbud	Late Apr-May	54-68
Carolina Rhododendron	Late Apr-June	308-310, 404-411
Dogwood	May	6, 85.8 PA, 154.5 PA, 230-232, 217-219, 378-282
Large-Flowered Trillium	May	3-7, 64-85, 154.5 PA, 168-169, 175, 330-340, 370-375
Fraser Magnolia	May	173-174, 252-253
Bluets	May-June	200.2, 355-368 PA
Wild Geranium	May-June	84-86, 170-172, 211.6, 375
Flame Azalea	May-June	138.6, 144-145, 149.5, 164-166, 217-221, 308-310, 368-380, 412-423
Fire Pink	May-June	1-2, 85.8 PA, 154.5 241 PA, 339.3 PA, 367-375, 404-408
Dodder or Love Vine	Aug-Sep	Common along roadside
Phlox	May-July	4, 79-82, 163-164, 200-202, 219-221, 339.3 PA, 370-380
Columbine	May-July	74-75, 339.3 PA, 370-378
Queen Anne's Lace	May-Sep	Common along open fields and roadside
Virginia Spiderwort	Late May-July	85.8 Sharp Top Trail, 380-381
Mountain Laurel	Late May-June	130.5, 162.9, 347.9, 380, 400
Catawba Rhododendron	June	44.9, 77-83, 130.5, 138.6, 239, 247, 266.8, 348-350, 364.1
Sundrop	June	8-10, 89-91, 229, 270.6, 351-352, 355-360, 370-375
Butterfly Weed	June-Aug	63-65, 238-246
White Rhododendron	June-July	162.9, 169 PA, 232-233, 339.3 PA, 352-353, 455-456
Deptford Pink	June-Aug	Common along grassy roadsides
Turk's Cap Lily	June-Aug	187.6, 364-368, 406-411
Mullein	June-Sep	Common along roadside on dry banks
Bull Thistle	Late June-frost	Common along roads & pastures at lower elevations
Fleabane	July	Common in fields and along roadside
Ox-Eye Daisy	July	Common in fields and along roadside
Yarrow	July	Common in fields and along roadside
Black-Eyed Susan	July	Common in fields and along roadside
Bergamot Bee Balm	July-Aug	38.8, 368-374
Tall Coneflower	July-Aug	36, 161.2, 228.1, 314, 359-368
Oswego Tea	July-Aug	Common in wet areas at higher elevations
White Snakeroot	July-Oct	Common along roadside
Jewelweed	Aug	Common along roadside in wet areas
Ironweed	Aug	245, 248
Joe-Pye Weed	Aug	6, 85.8 PA, 146, 248, 339.3 PA, 357-359
Cardinal Flower	Aug	Infrequently in wet places
Goldenrod	Sep	Common in fields and along roadside
Aster	Sep	Common in fields and along roadside

Spiderwort

Violet

Jewelweed

Fire Pink

PHOTOS BY JESSIE M. HARRIS   *Goldenrod*

Climate and Weather

Spring
It's springtime in the lowlands, winter in the mountains, or you can enjoy a second spring a month later at higher elevations. The weather's unpredictable: A sunny day can turn into a windy, bitterly cold one.

Summer
The blue haze that gives the mountains their name is created when sunshine and warm, humid air combine with the organic compounds (hydrocarbons) given off by the trees. Highest peaks see temps only to 70s.

Fall
This is the driest season, with warm, sunny days followed by crisp, clear nights. It's that combination of lack of rain and the warm/cool weather contrast that helps create the beauty of the leaf season.

Winter
Normally cold and clear, the weather can range from sunny and 70° (though rarely) to snowy and 20° with fog and clouds freezing into rime ice. High-peak extremes include sub-zero temperatures.

● For Parkway weather roadway info call (828) 298-0398. Sections of the parkway close to cars in winter due to weather.

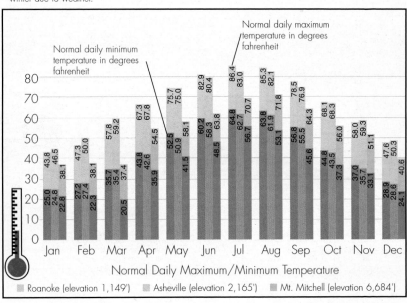

Normal daily maximum temperature in degrees fahrenheit

Normal daily minimum temperature in degrees fahrenheit

Normal Daily Maximum/Minimum Temperature

Roanoke (elevation 1,149')   Asheville (elevation 2,165')   Mt. Mitchell (elevation 6,684')

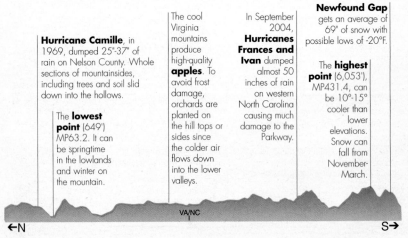

Hurricane Camille, in 1969, dumped 25"-37" of rain on Nelson County. Whole sections of mountainsides, including trees and soil slid down into the hollows.

The **lowest point** (649') MP63.2. It can be springtime in the lowlands and winter on the mountain.

The cool Virginia mountains produce high-quality **apples**. To avoid frost damage, orchards are planted on the hill tops or sides since the colder air flows down into the lower valleys.

In September 2004, **Hurricanes Frances and Ivan** dumped almost 50 inches of rain on western North Carolina causing much damage to the Parkway.

Newfound Gap gets an average of 69" of snow with possible lows of -20°F.

The **highest point** (6,053'), MP431.4, can be 10°-15° cooler than lower elevations. Snow can fall from November-March.

VA/NC

←N   S→